Design Thinking in Software and AI Projects

Proving Ideas Through Rapid Prototyping

Robert Stackowiak
Tracey Kelly

Apress®

Design Thinking in Software and AI Projects: Proving Ideas Through Rapid Prototyping

Robert Stackowiak
Elgin, IL, USA

Tracey Kelly
Parker, IN, USA

ISBN-13 (pbk): 978-1-4842-6152-1
https://doi.org/10.1007/978-1-4842-6153-8

ISBN-13 (electronic): 978-1-4842-6153-8

Managing Director, Apress Media LLC: Welmoed Spahr
Acquisitions Editor: Jonathan Gennick
Development Editor: Laura Berendson
Coordinating Editor: Jill Balzano

Cover image designed by Freepik (www.freepik.com)

Distributed to the book trade worldwide by Springer Science+Business Media New York, 233 Spring Street, 6th Floor, New York, NY 10013. Phone 1-800-SPRINGER, fax (201) 348-4505, e-mail orders-ny@springer-sbm.com, or visit www.springeronline.com. Apress Media, LLC is a California LLC and the sole member (owner) is Springer Science + Business Media Finance Inc (SSBM Finance Inc). SSBM Finance Inc is a **Delaware** corporation.

For information on translations, please e-mail booktranslations@springernature.com; for reprint, paperback, or audio rights, please e-mail bookpermissions@springernature.com.

Apress titles may be purchased in bulk for academic, corporate, or promotional use. eBook versions and licenses are also available for most titles. For more information, reference our Print and eBook Bulk Sales web page at http://www.apress.com/bulk-sales.

Any source code or other supplementary material referenced by the author in this book is available to readers on GitHub via the book's product page, located at www.apress.com/9781484261521. For more detailed information, please visit http://www.apress.com/source-code.

Printed on acid-free paper

To Jodie, my partner over these many years,
who makes solving life's problems fun.

—Robert Stackowiak

To Dan, my husband, who shares my consuming passion for user
experience design, and my parents who encouraged my love of
technology and creativity.

—Tracey Kelly

Table of Contents

About the Authors

Robert Stackowiak works as an independent consultant, advisor, and author. He is a former data and artificial intelligence architect and technology business strategist at the Microsoft Technology Center in Chicago and previously worked in similar roles at Oracle and IBM. He has conducted business discovery workshops, ideation workshops, and technology architecture sessions with many of North America's most leading-edge companies across a variety of industries and with government agencies. Bob has also spoken at numerous industry conferences internationally, served as a guest instructor at various universities, and is an author of several books. You can follow him on Twitter (@rstackow) and read his articles and posts on LinkedIn.

Tracey Kelly is the Envisioning Lead with the Catalyst team at Microsoft. She has been leading the Design Thinking training through North America and Europe to help Microsoft technology-focused architects and business leadership transition and transform to customer-centric and business outcome solutions. Tracey is also on the board of the Women's Technology Coalition and a former Women in Technology Director in Dallas. She leads design workshops and customer strategy sessions and has a long 20-year history of technology and design leadership at Fortune 500 companies to drive innovation.

Acknowledgments

We are obviously not the first to write about Design Thinking. Because previous practitioners shared their methodologies and approaches to problem identification and solution definition, we were able to learn from the best and adapt the exercises, tools, and methods into repeatable engagements appropriate to drive software and AI projects. We list many of these sources in the Appendix of this book and encourage you to investigate them as well.

Over the past few years, we worked in Microsoft Technology Centers and with the Microsoft Catalyst team in implementing many of these best practices. As we delivered Design Thinking training within Microsoft, we discovered many other practitioners of this approach within these groups and within Microsoft's partner community. We would like to thank some of the early proponents of applying this methodology there, including Craig Dillon, Carsten Scheumann, Shawna Flemming, Jennifer Kim, Jason Haggar, April Walker, Beth Malloy, Muge Wood, Charles Drayton, Dave Wentzel, Valerie Bergman, Sumit Wadhwa, Brandon Hancock, Jeff Hall, Daniel Hunter, Ryan McGann, Lafayette Howell, Kate Michel, Kevin Hughes, David Brown, Paul McPherson, Kevin Sharp, Harsh Panwar, Rob Nehrbas, Ruba Hachim, Amir Karim, J.P. DeCuire, Lora Lindsey, Susan Slagle, Sean McGuire, Nini Roed, Chris Han, Rudy Dillenseger, Ryan Hastings, Ovetta Sampson, Howe Gu, Aric Wood, and Thor Schueler.

As we were fine-tuning our techniques, we led workshops involving clients from a variety of industries who faced many different and often unique challenges. Those experiences helped us determine what worked and how to customize engagements for unique circumstances. Our thanks to those clients for enthusiastically taking part as we learned together. Hopefully, many of them continue to use Design Thinking as an approach today within their organizations.

The fine folks at Apress have once again provided us with an excellent writing and publishing experience. As he usually does, Jonathan Gennick, Assistant Editorial Director, helped us improve the book's original proposal by making excellent suggestions regarding content and guided the book through the approval process there. Jill Balzano,

ACKNOWLEDGMENTS

Coordinating Editor, helped us stage content and managed the review process behind the scenes. Having worked with other publishers where turnover is frequent, having these two consistently involved throughout the production of this book (and several others) is sincerely appreciated and speaks to the quality of the publisher.

Robert would like to thank Jodie, his wife of over 40 years. She has grown familiar with the dedicated time that must be spent writing books like this one (since he has been writing books for over 20 years). Her support and patience are truly amazing.

Next, Tracey would like to thank Robert for his friendship and collaborating on this book. Tracey would like to thank her friends Naomi, Rebecca, Wayne, Dennis, Erin, Jason, Mel, and Bri for constantly supporting her diverse creative endeavors no matter how crazy. Tracey deeply thanks and appreciates her mom and dad for always encouraging her to be creative and to invent/make things, to explore the world, to be curious about new technology, and to see failures or mistakes as opportunities to learn and grow.

Tracey would also like to thank Dan Kelly, her husband, who also has a love for thoughtful, well-designed products and services. He works in design as a product manager at Charles Schwab and has a passion for business education. She is deeply thankful for his support. He is truly a model for investing time to deeply understand the problem before jumping to solutions and not reacting. His kindness, wisdom, learner mindset, and integrity make him her favorite person in the world.

Introduction

We, the authors of this book, are on a journey. During much of our careers, we helped organizations define software, analytics, and AI technology footprints that were to be put into place to solve business problems. Some of those clients succeeded in building the solutions, rolling them out, and gaining widespread adoption. Others stumbled. Most often, when failure occurred, it was not due to the technology choices that were made.

Many technology people understand that the success rate of software development projects is not as high as it needs to be. The community has tried to solve this lack of success in various ways over many years. Most recently, there has been an emphasis on development in shorter cycles manned by small teams leveraging reusable services. The limited sprints in a modern DevOps approach can identify bad technology choices and unsuccessful development efforts sooner. However, this approach doesn't solve the problem of misguided efforts due to bad assumptions about what the business wants or needs.

Both of us spent significant time in recent years in front of business *and* IT audiences (including executives, managers, frontline workers, and developers/data scientists). When we got them together in the same room, magic began to happen. We were able to mediate discussions that provided a translation between what the business needed and what IT thought they wanted. Project goals became better defined, and success criteria became understood by all.

As we found our way, Design Thinking gained in popularity as a technique to be used in problem identification and solution definition. It was often applied where organizations were seeking to develop innovative processes and products. Today, this approach is taught in many leading universities and is practiced by a variety of consulting companies.

Where software is concerned, Design Thinking is most closely associated with user experience (UX) design of interfaces. However, we have found great value in using the technique to drive a much broader array of software and AI projects in our many client engagements.

INTRODUCTION

As we gathered our own best practices, we researched Design Thinking books and guides that targeted all sorts of design projects. Over time, we've adopted a core group of exercises and approaches that we find useful in our workshops that more often (than not) lead to software and AI projects.

This book is primarily focused on these best practices as we describe what Design Thinking is, preparing for a Design Thinking workshop, problem definition, and solution definition in the first four chapters. As we proceed through the workshop content, we apply our favorite methods and tools in a step-by-step fashion. To help you understand the output expected in each exercise, we illustrate sample output we might obtain in defining a supply chain optimization problem and potential solution.

In the remaining chapters, we proceed through software and AI prototype development, production development, and production rollout. We felt it important to show how the development process that follows the workshop is linked and note where we believe it could make sense to reexamine the conclusions and information that we found in the workshop.

We believe that Design Thinking is critical to defining the destination that an organization wants to reach and why it needs to go there. Starting a software development or AI project without this knowledge can result in many wrong turns and possibly lead nowhere. Investing in the time it takes to run a Design Thinking workshop should become part of an organization's standard operating procedures for any design. But we believe this to be especially true for software and AI projects where the goal is to deliver business value quickly, gain widespread adoption, avoid missteps, and minimize wasted efforts and resources.

CHAPTER 1

Design Thinking Overview and History

Does innovation come from a big idea that comes to an organization's leadership in the shower? Does it only come from the organization's extremely creative people? Does innovation only happen within dedicated innovation teams? Does it take a lot of money to innovate? The answer to all those questions is – not necessarily. If you want to truly innovate by developing next-level ideas, you need to think differently about how you approach innovation.

Many companies are in a rush for the next big idea out of fear of being disrupted, losing market share, or losing their business' differentiated value. We are all too familiar with businesses that didn't innovate well or fast enough, such as Blockbuster, Kodak, Nokia, Motorola, Borders, Atari, Commodore, BlackBerry, RadioShack, Netscape, AOL, Myspace, and many more. These companies couldn't react to changing business conditions fast enough to retain significant importance among their customers.

Surveys and news articles often note the increasing rate of change in named companies that appear in the Fortune 500 and the frequent disappearance of many of them. We note some of these surveys and articles in the Appendix listing sources for this book. Research into the financial statements of many companies further identifies disruption from non-traditional competition as providing additional risk to their businesses.

Much has been written lately about the strategic value that design and Design Thinking can add to organizations of any scale and type. Some articles and studies even cite a direct correlation between revenue growth and Design Thinking. Thus, Design Thinking has gained momentum in the business world and is mentioned in many publications including those from the Design Management Institute, the *Harvard Business Review*, and *Forbes*.

R. Stackowiak and T. Kelly, *Design Thinking in Software and AI Projects*

In this chapter, we provide you with an introduction to Design Thinking. The topics we cover are as follows:

- Design Thinking and innovation

- Overcoming fear of failure

- Approach is everything

- A brief history and frameworks

- Design Thinking, DevOps, and adoption

- Summary

Design Thinking and Innovation

Design Thinking is an innovation technique that can be adopted by anyone, anywhere, and at little to no cost. It is a problem-solving technique that can be applied to small or large problems. It can be used to address business or non-business problems.

Most people think that innovation requires one to be an artist or highly creative. In our experience, we have heard people we are training to conduct these workshops say, "I'm not really a creative person" or "I'm not an artist."

According to Alice Flaherty, an American neurologist and author of *The Midnight Disease*, "A creative idea is defined simply as one that is both novel and useful (or influential) in a particular social setting." Flaherty explains that this applies to every field, including programming, business, mathematics, and the traditional "creative" fields, like music or drawing.

Thus, Design Thinking and innovation are very misunderstood. Many people believe that innovation occurs when brilliant ideas spring out of nowhere or that innovation requires the right creative personality type or the right team of people and skills. While these conditions can be beneficial and some people do use time in the shower or when they are half asleep to come up with great ideas, Design Thinking is a much more widely inclusive approach.

The Design Thinking approach to innovation combines intent, exploration, and the views of a diverse group of people. People taking part should have an open mindset and be willing to fail in order to learn. More brains working on a problem enables focus on the problem from different perspectives and results in creation of a multitude of possible solutions. Diverse groups of people can think about and sort out complex problems, even when they haven't experienced the problem before or have limited information or context about the problem.

The mind is an amazing problem-solving organ. There are different parts of the brain that are activated when intentionally focused on a problem (prefrontal cortex) vs. not focused on a problem (anterior cingulate cortex). Our brains are always working on sorting out challenges and problem, even when we aren't focused on it.[1]

The belief that innovation can spring out of anywhere is true, but it's way more valuable and exciting when used to solve a critical or pressing problem. As Plato has stated, "Necessity is literally the mother of all invention." A need or a challenge is the spark that ignites the imagination to create and invent ways of solving a problem. Additionally, one idea alone is good, but the power of multiple ideas to solve a problem exponentially increases solution quality.

The authors believe that the first idea generated isn't always the best idea. A volume of ideas or solutions promotes the opportunity for careful consideration of the best fit to solve a problem. It can take many people to create the needed volume even in situations where some individuals are gifted in creating such volume.

In *Buzan's Book of Genius* (1994), Leonardo da Vinci was ranked in first place for the top ten thinkers of all time. da Vinci was a prolific inventor that was truly ahead of his time because he was great at thinking and pondering problems and considered a variety of ways to solve those problems. He was a thinker and prolific sketcher. Of the 13,000 pages of sketches of images and ideas, he only had 30 finished paintings and 16 inventions, but some have changed history forever. Among da Vinci's notable inventions are

- Parachute

- Diving suit

- Armored tank

- Flying machine/glider

- Machine gun

According to the book *How to Think Like Leonardo da Vinci: Seven Steps to Genius Every Day*, we should be curious, test knowledge, learn from mistakes, improve our experiences, embrace ambiguity or paradox, use whole brain thinking, use the physical

---

[1]The brain and problem-solving: https://study.com/academy/lesson/the-brain-problem-solving-areas-process.html

world, and see the interconnections between things. Specifically, we should use the creative and evaluative sides of our brains to solve challenges.

Picasso was a prolific producer of artwork with 147,800 completed projects. Picasso once said, "Give me a museum and I will fill it up." The Louvre exhibits 35,000 pieces of art; thus, he could fill this museum more than four times over. But not every one of his pieces is in a museum. Quantity doesn't equal quality. But quantity ensures a better selection pool for the *best* ideas.

Many people think art is the same thing as design. While both share a need for creativity, they are not the same. Good art inspires and pushes one to ask questions, to ponder, to feel, and to respond with emotion and thought. Artists use their own perspectives, feelings, emotion, insight, and experiences to create, but their creations do not need to solve problems or answer questions. Rather, their creations pose them.

In comparison, design's purpose is to function well in solving problems. Design has both purpose and intent. It must meet requirements to be successful, and it must serve a purpose in order to derive value. Good design is more restrained and focused on the best way to solve a problem so many draft versions or iterations are typically created and tested before a final solution is employed.

Everything is designed – cars, chairs, tables, clothes, software, roads, services … everything. Thus, adopting Design Thinking can be a widely applicable and powerful tool.

When organizations build products and services, some don't realize they need to include in their designs how to attract, retain, and support their clients and customers. Lack of thoughtful design is still design, but it is neglected design. Good design is outcome-oriented and process-driven. The intent guides the process and direction, but the path taken should be very flexible and considered a learning opportunity.

Overcoming Fear of Failure

Many people fear a structured approach to design because they don't want to fail. They are afraid to start because they want their design to be perfect. Perfection paralysis is a real problem for many. It can stop many entrepreneurs and software developers from doing anything.

Failure is a recognized ingredient in Design Thinking. It is seen as presenting an opportunity to learn what doesn't work. Designs evolve using new insights and parameters that failures uncover. Thus, one needs to embrace failure as part of the process.

Failure using this approach is sometimes referred to as failing forward. As John C. Maxwell writes in *Failing Forward: Turning Mistakes into Stepping Stones for Success*, "I want to help you learn how to confidently look the prospect of failure in the eye and move forward anyway... Because in life, the question is not *if* you will have problems, but how you are going to deal with them. Stop failing backward and start *failing forward*!"

Innovative design should be a purposeful learning opportunity with the expectation that you won't get it right on the first try. It likely won't feature gifted artistry, perfection, or a clear upfront definition. However, it does require a thoughtful and creative approach to problem-solving that we are going to discuss throughout this book.

During our lives, solving problems is how we experience the world. From our first moment of learning to walk, eat, and play, there are problems to be solved. Early learning challenges such as how one should move, where one might go, where one places a foot when walking, and how one makes shapes with a pencil to write letters or words are examples of areas where we make mistakes and eventually succeed. Those incremental steps in problem-solving are what helps us learn new skills.

As we age, the challenges become more complex. Examples include social situations, applying for and keeping jobs, financial responsibilities, and physical challenges. All these provide opportunities to learn and grow.

When we face business challenges, collective teams working to solve problems might appear to increase complexity. But a richer base of experience grows as teams learn from failure, adapt to new insights, and evolve their thinking to make things, processes, and people better. Design Thinking is all about improvements – making things better, more useful, more functional, more beautiful, more usable, more valuable, and/or more important.

Approach Is Everything

Since one can choose from many approaches to solving problems, some tend to go with what has worked for them in the past. However, not all past experiences produce the best results. The authors believe that some approaches are productive while others are not. The approach used, either individually or as a team, impacts the results and efficacy of the solution produced and must be taken seriously.

Behavior and psychology play a big role in Design Thinking and problem-solving and can impact individuals or a whole team dynamic. Before embarking on the Design Thinking journey, consider the benefits of taking a productive approach over one considered as non-productive.

A non-productive approach can result in missed opportunities for success, frustration, less impactful results, solving for the wrong problem, dissention in teams, a breakdown in communication, and not partly or fully solving the problem. Bias might come from a single person or from the collective group. One should try to identify any of these signs early and instead adopt a creative, proactive, curious, humble, and service-oriented mindset.

Non-productive approaches to solving problems include

- Reactionary – Taking the first idea and going with it

- Isolative – One person believing their expertise is the only way to solve a problem

- Indecisive – Spending too much time on the problem and having the inability to decide (also known as analysis paralysis)

- Stalling/avoiding – Deciding not to solve a problem now and hoping that it might go away despite evidence to the contrary

- Prejudice – Bias in favor of one thing, person, group, or idea without the consideration of other ideas or opinions

- Persecuting – Using blame, anger, and aggression to persuade, defend, or argue to an idea or solution that benefits that one person or group

- Victimizing – Complaining without solving and denying responsibility/ownership of the problem and dwelling on complaints vs. solutions

- Rescuing – Taking on all the responsibility for solving problems regardless of boundaries and solving problems out of fear, resentment, or a self-serving desire to be needed and not including or holding others responsible

Productive approaches to solving problems include

- Contemplative – Prolonged thought processes with the intent to weigh all the options carefully before deciding by using critical thinking, specifically analyzing and assessing pros and cons and patterns for success or failure

- Curious – Research unknown areas shining light upon blind spots to uncover additional information

- Empathetic – Understand and share the feelings of the individuals and teams who experience the current problem and will be impacted by the future solution

- Collaborative – Using a group of people to solve a challenge who have different ideas, perspectives, opinions, or investment stakes in the solution

- Diverse – Gathering a mix of perspectives and views that challenge the value, benefit, and status quo impacts of various ideas generated

- Contextual – Using people who are affected by or impacted by the change

- Challenging – Using healthy conflict to ensure the best possible solution can occur – not to be mistaken for bullying behavior – but healthy and productive debate

The way you approach solving problems can affect the outcome or solution you end up with. Design Thinking employs productive and systematic methods. It requires more than one person to consider the problem more thoroughly prior to jumping into considering solutions.

Note   The authors believe that Albert Einstein had it right when he said, "If I had an hour to solve a problem, I'd spend 55 minutes thinking about the problem and five minutes thinking about solutions."

While Design Thinking can be done by anyone and can be done anywhere at minimal cost, it requires teams with dedicated time to think, discuss, and define problems carefully before working on solutions. It enables and encourages collaborative understanding and alignment and ownership of problems and solutions and drives ownership of next steps.

The recommended size of the teams varies from two to twenty people. However, keep in mind that as more people take part, it will take more time for groups to hear everyone's ideas. The ideal or optimal group size in our opinion is four to eight people. All voices can be heard in conversations without taking too long, and ideas and concepts can be tested more rapidly. As an additional benefit, it can be inexpensive to feed them with a pizza or two!

A Brief History and Frameworks

Design Thinking developed as an approach to problem-solving beginning in the 1950s within the industrial design, science, and technology communities. In the 1960s, inclusive and collaborative problem-solving began to replace a closed-off and selective approach. Gathering of user feedback in the design process became popular. Increased usage of computers and technology led to the start of human-computer interaction design in the 1970s.

Beginning in the 1990s, a shift to specialization within the design process made its presence apparent as the so-called wicked problems in Design Thinking. In 1991, IDEO was formed as a company, resulting from a three-way merger, and invited diverse experts from anthropology, business strategy, and other disciplines to create design teams.

For the past 20 years, the Design Thinking approach and its ability to drive innovation in business and drive revenue has caught the eyes of many executives. A variety of *frameworks* have appeared that define the phases and steps used in Design Thinking engagements and workshops (as a search for "Design Thinking" via an Internet search engine will readily demonstrate).

Each framework should be evaluated for its effectiveness in solving your problems and for your situations. Additionally, the methods and time spent within each phase of a framework might also be different from project to project. You could find that you might go in reverse or skip phases depending how the problem and information unfolds.

Keep in mind that a framework is simply that. It should be flexible to bend to what you need and help to drive proper outcomes. Additionally, the methods within each phase of the framework should be just as flexible.

Methods can be thought of as exercises or activities that produce insight or information. There are thousands of methods that can be applied within each phase, and each phase is subjective to the outcome you need to achieve. For example, in the Stanford d.school framework (described in the next subsection), you could use a persona, empathy map, interviews, surveys, and data on website visits or do shadowing to gain outcomes involving a group of people during the define phase.

Each method will yield only a portion of information needed. Interviews provide qualitative data such as sentiment or why someone does something. But you might not see hard numbers or facts. With surveys, you will get the numbers and quantitative facts, but not the why. Carefully consider what information you need before you invest time, money, and resource in a method that doesn't yield the full view of results and information you need for decision-making.

Stanford d.school Framework

As you might expect given Stanford University's long history of teaching Design Thinking in its Institute of Design, it has defined one of the more popular frameworks being used. Key phases in the Stanford d.school framework are empathize, define, ideate, prototype, and test. These are illustrated in the diagram in Figure 1-1.

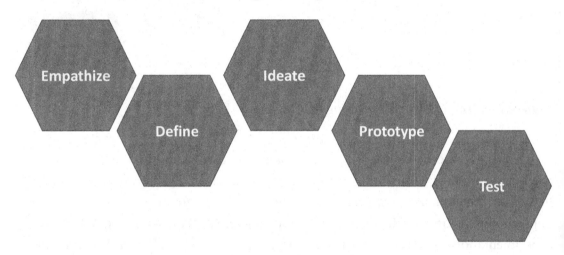

Figure 1-1. *Stanford d.school Design Thinking framework*

During the empathize phase, the focus is on interviews, shadowing, seeking to understand, and non-judgmental methods. In the define phase, the focus moves to understanding personas, role objectives, decisions, challenges, and pain points. In the ideate phase, ideas are shared, all ideas might be considered worthy, a diverge and converge method can be used, ideas might be extended using a "Yes and" method, and prioritization frequently takes place. During the prototype phase, mockups and storyboards might be created, a "keep it simple" approach might be applied, and methods of failing fast and quickly iterating might also be applied. In the testing phase, gaining an understanding of impediments, an understanding of what works, evaluating tests through role-plays, and performing tests in fast iterations are the methods that might be used.

IDEO Framework

Another popular framework is IDEO's Design Thinking methodology. Key phases in this framework are discovery, interpretation, ideation, experimentation, and evolution. These are illustrated in Figure 1-2 using a representation like that in Figure 1-1 so that you can see the similarity to the Stanford d.school version.

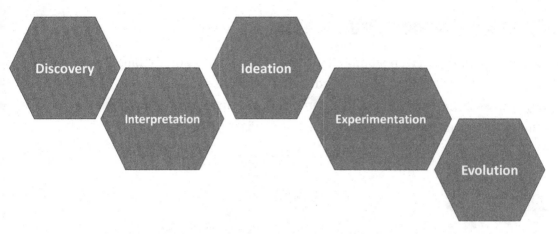

Figure 1-2. *IDEO Design Thinking framework*

During the discovery phase, the focus is on understanding the approach to a challenge by understanding what it is, preparing research, and gathering inspiration. In the interpretation phase, stories are told, there is a search for meaning, and opportunities are framed. In ideation, creation ideas are generated and refined. The experimentation phase consists of making prototypes and getting feedback. Evolution includes tracking learnings and moving forward.

Double Diamond Design Methodology

At the heart of the original framework that most other innovative design frameworks are based upon is the UK Design Council's design methodology, the Double Diamond – a clear, comprehensive, and visual description of the design process. Launched in 2004, the Double Diamond has become world-renowned with millions of references to it on the Web. (See the Appendix for a reference that we used in this book.)

The Design Council's Double Diamond clearly conveys a design process to designers and non-designers alike. We illustrate the Double Diamond in Figure 1-3.

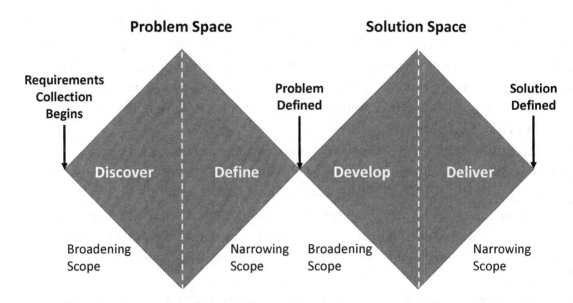

Figure 1-3. *Double Diamond Design Thinking methodology*

The two diamonds represent the problem space and solution space in this approach. The left portion of each diamond represents a process of exploring an issue more widely or deeply (divergent thinking), while the right portion of each diamond represents taking focused action (convergent thinking).

Key *phases* in the Double Diamond are discover, define, develop, and deliver. Discover and define are part of the problem space, while develop and deliver are part of the solution space. The phases are fixed within this methodology; however, the *objectives* or intent within these phases can change depending upon what we know (or don't know).

Within the problem space diamond, we gain an understanding, rather than simply assuming, what the problem is. We begin collecting requirements within the discover phase. Typical objectives in this phase include

- Setting scope – Defining an initial problem or vision statement

- Determining people/stakeholders – Who is impacted or influenced

- Determining what is the current state – Good or bad

During the define phase, we seek to understand what problem we really need to solve for. The insight that we gained from the discovery phase should help us to define this challenge in a new way, and we should leave this phase with our problem much better defined. It is important to remember that the first problem that was identified might not be the most important problem to solve for. We must also understand why solving a specific problem really matters.

We are now ready to enter the solution space. We focus in the design phase on ideating on ways to solve the defined problem. Our diverse attendees are encouraged to provide a wide variety of potential solutions. During the determine phase that follows, we prioritize these solutions around their value and effort required. We then begin to iteratively test the ideas to figure out which one(s) might work and would be best to improve upon and which ones will not. After going through these iterations, we will have a solution defined.

Solution design and determination is not a linear process. Many organizations learn something more about the underlying problems using this methodology, and this gained knowledge can send them back to the beginning. Making some assumptions and testing of early stage ideas can be part of discovery. And in an ever-changing and digital world, no idea is ever "finished." We are constantly getting feedback on how products and services are working and iteratively improving them.

The design principles behind the framework describe four core principles for problem-solvers to adopt so that they can work as effectively as possible. These are

- Put people first – Start with an understanding of the people using a service, their needs, strengths, and aspirations.

- Communicate visually and inclusively – Help people gain a shared understanding of the problem and ideas.

- Collaborate and co-create – Work together and get inspired by what others are doing.

- Iterate, iterate, iterate – Do this to spot errors early, avoid risk, and build confidence in your ideas.

The Design Council has authored, adapted, or adopted a portfolio of design methods, which help clients to identify and address their challenges and achieve successful outcomes. They have structured these methods in three areas to help in using the design process to explore, shape, or build in order to create a culture of success:

- Explore – Challenges, needs, and opportunities

- Shape – Prototypes, insights, and visions

- Build – Ideas, plans, and expertise

So, you might now be wondering which framework to choose and what methods and approaches might be applied to meet your own objectives.

Applying a Framework and Methodology

The problems that we face today commonly require the ideas and buy-in from diverse stakeholders who must also be part of the solution. Equal in importance to the process and principles we adopt is the culture of the organization and how it connects with consumers/citizens and its business partners.

Leadership is needed to encourage innovation, build skills and capability, and provide permission for experimentation and learning. Strong leadership also allows projects to be open and agile, showing results along the way and being able to change.

Engagement is needed with people who are delivering the ideas and receiving them, but also with other partners who might have other ideas. Developing these connections and building relationships is as important as creating ideas.

If you line up all the frameworks and methodologies, you will notice they are similar with subtle differences. For the purposes of cohesiveness in this book, we will use the Double Diamond as our standard when referencing a singular methodology.

The alignment is also reflected in our recommended methods (activities, exercises, and outputs) that can be employed in each phase of the Double Diamond framework. We will walk you through some of the popular methods for meeting objectives aligned to the problem space in Chapter 3 and aligned to the solution space in Chapter 4 of this book.

Design Thinking, DevOps, and Adoption

Design Thinking helps organizations discern unmet needs, create value from these insights, and create competitive advantages. Today, it is often used in conjunction with the DevOps approach adopted by many software and AI developers.

While DevOps has helped teams of developers organize around their development challenges, Design Thinking helps businesses solve real business complex challenges using innovation. Change is hard for many, but Design Thinking gives order to chaos. It's a way to navigate, explore, and test ideas to ensuring value, business viability, and technical feasibility. Combining the two approaches fosters a collaborative and user-centered culture with an iterative approach to fail forward with change.

In the past, innovation was often approached from the top down. This approach was omnidirectional and not very scalable at any level. Incorporating Design Thinking removes silos, invites healthy conflict in discussion to challenge the norms, and creates ideas that are valuable. These, in turn, help businesses create revenue and deliver customer and/or employee satisfaction.

Many organizations do not do this well. The transition to Design Thinking needs to be driven from an executive level to help build innovative design into an organization's DNA. It should trickle down into every software or AI project being considered along with the challenges those project charters are trying to solve.

How long might such cultural change take? Leveraging some earlier work by Jakob Nielsen, Gena Drahun estimated the average time it would take to develop a user-driven culture in 2015. According to Drahun, the typical phases and adoption periods are as follows:

- Stage 1 – Developer-centered

- Stage 2 – Skunkworks (2 years)

- Stage 3 – Dedicated budget (4 years)

- Stage 4 – Managed (7 years)

- Stage 5 – Systematic process (13 years)

- Stage 6 – Integrated user-centered design (20 years)

- Stage 7 – User-driven corporation (40 years)

However, in the authors' view, proven benefits from leveraging a Design Thinking approach (and the necessity to react more quickly to emerging business challenges) are helping to speed adoption in many organizations. In Chapter 7, we describe how change management is an important part of speeding this adoption.

One advantage to using a Design Thinking approach is that it helps an organization more deeply understand the root cause of problems, the contributing factors, context, and reasons for the problem. Learning about the cause can sometimes point to a solution. Such insight may not have been available during earlier approaches used in addressing the problem.

Design Thinking also creates a sense of ownership for the teams working in collaboration to help solve the problem. This unified approach can create alignment. Specifically, as the team works together to understand and clarify various points of information, perspectives, opinions, and thoughts, they can synthesize the information in to a collective and more holistic point of view.

Additionally, Design Thinking ensures that the final product, service, or solution meets the initial objectives or client requirements. Since part of the process is defining success and testing if ideas deliver success, the value of results is ensured. Since Design Thinking is iterative, continuous iterative loops through changing information, ideation, validation, and implementation can result in a continuous improvement process that builds on the success and failure of the last iteration.

The ultimate benefit is the solution continually gets better as more information, knowledge, and ideas are applied.

Summary

As we come to the end of this chapter, you should better understand how Design Thinking helps organizations identify and solve problems more rapidly and helps drive innovation. You should also see how this iterative approach provides a means to get beyond setbacks that occur in projects and use those setbacks as learning experiences.

You should now recognize some keys to taking a productive approach (as well as some of the non-productive methods and approaches that should be avoided). You also had a brief introduction to popular frameworks that help ensure a productive approach will be taken. We'll explore methods and exercises in typical Design Thinking workshops in Chapters 3 and 4 that neatly align to the Double Diamond.

Finally, you should now think of Design Thinking as complementary to a modern DevOps approach. And you should understand its benefits and how those can help drive adoption.

We begin a deeper exploration of applying the methodology in Chapter 2 as we discuss preparing for a Design Thinking workshop.

CHAPTER 2

Preparing for a Workshop

Now that you understand how Design Thinking became an important tool in identifying problems to be solved and uncovering possible solutions, you are likely ready to use the methodology in strategy development. While some might associate Design Thinking workshops primarily with user experience (UX) design in software projects, these workshops are now also commonly used to define the full scope of the business solutions to be provided in comprehensive software and AI development projects. Your role in a Design Thinking workshop might include leading, sponsoring, or simply taking part in the workshop.

This chapter covers preparing for a Design Thinking workshop. We suggest how you might describe this workshop to others and provide a sample agenda. We also help you understand the key roles of individuals that should be present during a workshop, their responsibilities, some best practices when gathering the right participants, and initial rules and guidelines that should be conveyed to all.

Next, we provide some guidance particularly useful to facilitators of these workshops, including suggestions on possible prework research using a couple of popular formats that capture the state of the business. We also describe gathering intelligence about what could be top of mind in attendees and share our observations regarding current areas of solutioning focus across a broad set of industries. Finally, we provide a description of facility considerations and the supplies that should be gathered in preparation for a workshop.

Thus, major sections of this chapter are

- Conveying what the workshop is about

- Roles and responsibilities

- Coordination prior to the workshop

- Facilitation and independent research

- Top-of-mind industry topics

© Robert Stackowiak and Tracey Kelly 2020
R. Stackowiak and T. Kelly, *Design Thinking in Software and AI Projects*

- Workshop facility and supplies

- Summary

Conveying What the Workshop Is About

If you are positioning the value of a potential workshop to others and/or planning to facilitate the workshop, you should have a workshop description readily in mind. The following paragraph is one that the authors have used in describing what a Design Thinking workshop is.

> *A diverse group of business and technology stakeholders and potential users of software and AI solutions are brought together in a Design Thinking workshop to define and prioritize the challenges that they face and collaborate in an innovative fashion to determine possible solutions to those challenges. They share a common goal of driving significant business impact. A Design Thinking workshop typically takes place over a period of one or two days.*

The workshop sometimes leads to or is dovetailed with a technology architectural design session. Greater technical detail is gathered in this subsequent technology architectural design session leading to more clarity regarding what the potential solution might look like and who will need to take part in building it.

Regardless of whether greater in-depth technology definition takes place initially, those who take part in the Design Thinking workshop should walk away with a clear action plan and understand the critical next steps to moving the project forward. You might further describe benefits of the workshop as follows:

- Creates alignment by gathering a diverse team that breaks down silos in an organization and unifies exploration of problems and solutions

- Provides a highly interactive experience that assures engagement of all interested parties present

- Leads to new insight by collaboratively looking at problems, solutions, and potential impacts at a deeper level from many diverse points of view

- For all engaged, creates a feeling of ownership of the problems and solutions that are identified in the workshop (each person develops a vested interest in addressing what is uncovered)

Simply indicating that a Design Thinking approach will be used can lead interested parties to go to their favorite search engine to find out what this is all about. (This seems to be particularly true for technology-oriented participants.) However, if you are promoting or facilitating the workshop, you might also be asked to provide a typical agenda that describes the flow of the workshop. Such an agenda would include key Double Diamond approach exercises and methods and can look something like this:

1. Introductions and logistics

2. An introduction to Design Thinking

3. Establishing diverse teams for the workshop

4. A discussion/determination of the most important goal(s) of the organization

5. Creating a unified vision around the goal(s)

6. Choosing scope(s) to address the goal(s)

7. Creating a stakeholder map and describing personas of select stakeholders

8. Denoting positives, negatives, and opportunities for identified scope(s) and stakeholders

9. Transitioning to ideation through a "how might we" statement

10. Using a creative matrix to identify possible solutions

11. Placing solutions on a value-effort chart

12. Creating a storyboard/visualization

13. Further solution evaluation

14. Road map of next steps

We will dig deeper into these topics in subsequent chapters with guidance on how to participate in and facilitate these exercises.

Regardless of whether the facilitator provides an agenda, it should be made clear to all potential attendees that they need to be physically present to take part in the session.

Note   In our experience, we have had attendees decide to not be physically present in the workshop at the last minute. They typically ask for remote conferencing into the workshop, but when they observe the interactive nature of it, it soon becomes apparent to them that they needed to be physically present. They generally then decide to drop off the call and await the results of the workshop.

Roles and Responsibilities

Regardless of your role in the workshop, you can help to improve its outcome by helping to assure that a diverse group of participants are present from the organization. These include leadership and other participants from the lines of business, technologists, and support groups. In some situations, it can make sense for people external to the company to be present such as suppliers, distributors, or key customers. During the workshop itself, individuals serving in key roles of facilitator, proctor, and scribe will also be present.

Participants from the lines of business should have a specific business goal or goals in mind. A key executive sponsor or sponsors must be present during the workshop to share their vision and to also ensure that they will be fully brought into the solution(s) after the workshop ends. The sponsor(s) also have a key role in identifying users and external individuals closest to the problem(s) and can help ensure their participation.

Users and external individuals can provide a unique "frontline" perspective regarding the challenges being faced. As a result, they can be extremely important in also defining the kind(s) of solutions that might be most effective.

Technologists might come from the company that will use the solution, a consulting partner, and/or the vendor providing key software components. Examples of technologists who might participate include software developers, data scientists, data management systems architects and administrators, and IT infrastructure leaders. They should be present to answer technical questions during or after the workshop but should not be allowed to make recommendations unless specifically asked. During the workshop, their time is best spent focused on deep discovery with business executives and users to understand their needs and constraints, as well as the impacts and value of potential solutions.

Figure 2-1 provides an illustration representing the interaction among these key roles in defining problems and solutions in a Design Thinking workshop. This interaction is guided by a facilitator.

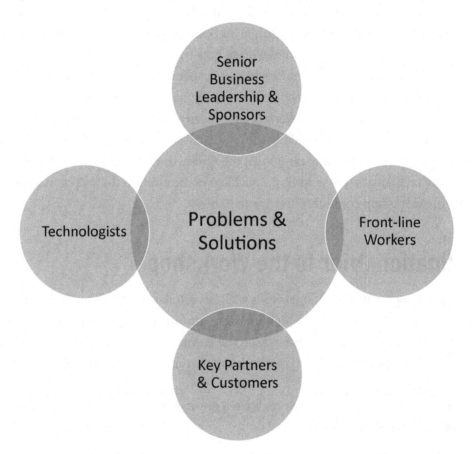

Figure 2-1. *Diverse roles typically present in Design Thinking workshops*

The workshop facilitator should be extremely familiar with best practices in Design Thinking. Within exceptionally large companies, there are sometimes individuals with such skills in their job descriptions. More commonly, these individuals are found within consulting organizations or certain software and cloud-based solutions vendors.

During the workshop, the facilitator has several important responsibilities in addition to reminding attendees of rules agreed upon prior to the workshop (see the next section in this chapter). Throughout the workshop, they coach individuals and teams through exercises aligned to the Double Diamond technique, helping them maintain focus on the tasks at hand. Experienced facilitators encourage the participants to fully explore options at each step while helping them get outside of their comfort zones in order to uncover critical information. They seek to spark curiosity and mediate discussions whenever necessary. The facilitator also manages time throughout the day, looks for signs of disengagement by individuals, and tries to assure clarity of ideas and outcomes during each exercise.

Proctors can assist the main facilitator by providing guidance to teams as they execute the exercises. The proctors might be less experienced than the main facilitator and sometimes use the proctoring role to learn how to better facilitate future engagements that they will conduct. Proctors are especially useful when there are many teams and/or the teams are exploring diverse problems and solutions.

Scribes are recommended in order to collect core analog content during the workshop. This can include note-taking during discussions and capturing content on whiteboards and easels by taking photos. At the end of the workshop, the scribe(s) work with the facilitator on assembling a package of the content that was generated and distribute the workshop content to the participants.

Coordination Prior to the Workshop

Prior to the workshop, the facilitator works with key sponsor(s) on identifying goals for the workshop and ensuring that the right participants are invited. The facilitator might also perform some independent research on the company's likely goals (as described in the next section of this chapter) and research the participants that are invited if they are unfamiliar with them.

A best practice is for the facilitator to have a pre-call with the sponsor(s) and/or key participants prior to the workshop to

- Define workshop value and outcomes

- Set guidelines and rules for the workshop

- Confirm the right participants will be present

- Ask for additional information

Define Workshop Value and Outcomes

The client may not be in full agreement that they need to disrupt normal work activities for several people for one to two days so that they can take part in a Design Thinking workshop. They might need additional information to better understand the workshop's goal, key activities, and expected output.

The overall goal and value of the workshop can be succinctly stated as getting everyone on the same page by sharing ideas that will lead to creative problem-solving and drive next steps to move forward. Key activities include

- Identification of a "north star" vision of where to focus improvements in the business

- Understanding problems within the business that are inhibiting success

- Defining how to measure success

- Empathizing with stakeholders who empower or hinder success

- Aligning teams to co-create/innovate ideas that drive needed outcomes

- Prioritizing the most impactful ideas into concepts that can be realized

- Defining the business impact and benefit and visualizing the solution(s)

Expected output gained from the workshop includes

- A clear agreed-upon vision of the future

- An understanding of the risk in maintaining the status quo

- Alignment regarding clearly defined success criteria

- Documented business and technical challenges from various perspectives

- Documented views of key stakeholders that impact solutions success

- Solution ideas to problems that are prioritized based on business impact and technical implementation efforts needed

- An action plan to move solution idea(s) forward with clear ownership, timelines, and next steps

Set Guidelines and Rules for the Workshop

The pre-call should also set expectations regarding the expected behavior of participants during the workshop. The facilitator should remind the sponsor that everyone should be aware of the following rules:

- Bring an open mindset to the workshop.

- Be physically present during the workshop.

- Laptops will be turned off and other mobile devices put away (if these are not being used for note-taking) as no email or texting unrelated to the workshop should be exchanged when it takes place.

- Exercises will be timed to keep the workshop on track.

- Any discussions determined out of scope during the workshop will be noted and deferred to an appropriate time.

These guidelines and rules are sometimes repeated in an email to all participants prior to the workshop date. As we mentioned earlier in this chapter, they are also typically repeated by the facilitator at the start of the workshop.

Confirm the Right Participants Will Be Present

Having an adequate number of individuals with a diversity of business backgrounds representing various goals and perceived problems in the organization will be critical. This diversity is key to driving innovative and comprehensive discussions in each of the teams created in the workshop. Key technology implementation participants should also be present to validate the feasibility of potential solutions from a technical perspective.

For example, when seeking to solve supply chain problems at a manufacturer of industrial equipment, here are some typical titles of individuals who could be present:

- VPs of manufacturing and transportation/logistics (sponsors)

- Managers of operations

- CFO

- Supply chain business analysts and data scientists

- Representatives from suppliers and distributors

- CIO

- IT supply chain management system software developers and managers

- Workshop facilitator

- Workshop proctor(s)

- Workshop scribe(s)

Ask for Additional Information

The facilitator should work with the sponsor to identify and gather prework to help facilitate exercises during the workshop. The content should be reviewed by the facilitator at least a week in advance of the workshop to consider how to incorporate it into the agenda. Some items that might be included in the prework include

- Areas that the client wants to focus upon, possibly including the biggest challenges motivating executives

- Workshop outcomes desired by the executive sponsor

- A list of primary stakeholders impacted by the defined areas of focus including their ability to attend the workshop, their areas of interest, and their incentives

- Their "service blueprint" that provides a customer/support/ operational view of their organization (and its relationship to their areas of focus)

- Any history they have with previous Design Thinking workshops or similar workshops and possible barriers to success

- The state of data associated with their areas of focus including completeness and quality

- General business challenges

- Topics, technologies, and areas of the business to avoid during the workshop

Facilitation and Independent Research

If you are a facilitator and are looking for areas of potential innovation to explore in a Design Thinking workshop, you will certainly start with goals brought forth by the sponsor(s) of the workshop. However, doing research on your own can be beneficial and is especially useful in driving out-of-the-box thinking among attendees.

You might start your research by reviewing recent mission statements, financial statements, and public presentations by the company or organization. There can sometimes be a disconnect between goals expressed by very senior leadership and the people you are talking with, so such research can shed light on potentially more far-reaching goals and current problems. You might also interview a broader group of individuals within the company or organization and seek candid suggestions and feedback.

Sometimes, it can be useful to research the backgrounds of the key proposed attendees by using tools such as LinkedIn or company/organization website profiles. Understanding the backgrounds of these individuals, including previous roles in driving innovative solutions, can help you understand the potential dynamics that will occur in a workshop.

It is worth noting that top-of-mind senior executive goals might also be driven by what leadership thinks their competition is up to and the perceived threats that competitors might soon present. These might include investments being made by competition in new and non-traditional business areas that could eventually lead the company to become a niche player. Focus your research on competitors' senior executive and leadership views published in news articles, annual reports and financial statements, and presentations at conferences. Through these, you can gain insight into new initiatives and potential risks that the competition sees in its business.

As you do your research, you might want to evaluate current political, economic, social, technological, environmental, and legal factors impacting the business. This is sometimes referenced as a PESTEL analysis and can help you understand some of influencing factors that might provide tailwinds or provoke headwinds during the Design Thinking workshop. Some examples of factors in each of these areas that could influence projects under consideration include

- Political factors such as organizational power structure, policies, stability of leadership and organization, existing agreements among different entities, and willingness to take risk and invest

- Economic factors such as market health, purchasing power of their clients, material costs, transportation and labor costs, amount of debt, rates of inflation and interest, and employment rates

- Social factors such as changing demographics, diversity of workers and clients, societal values, available skills and levels of education, and attitudes toward technology and data privacy

- Technological factors such as the diversity of data, quality of data, proliferation of data sources, flexibility and integration capabilities of existing systems and equipment, availability of artificial intelligence and machine learning compute resources, and rates of innovation present in similar competing companies and organizations

- Environmental factors such as energy utilization and availability, other raw material and natural resource considerations, impact on pollution and climate change, and ability to withstand extreme weather and other natural conditions and events

- Legal factors including local, national, and international laws and regulations, contracts, taxation, and liability implications

Another way of looking at an organization is by utilizing a business model canvas, first proposed by Alexander Osterwalder early in this century. Several variations of the business model canvas can be found on a variety of websites and publications (see the Appendix for references containing some examples). The business model canvas can be useful as we approach and begin the workshop and might also be used at the conclusion of the workshop when we have defined a solution.

Business model canvas key factors that we find useful in describing a company or organization capture the following:

- Value propositions that define what is being delivered as products or services to customers, clients, and/or constituents

- Customer/client/constituent segments that describe who products or services are being created for and which of the segments are targeted as being most important

- Customer/client/constituent relationships that describe current and desired relationships

- Channels that describe how the various segments are reached

- Key activities that describe how value propositions are delivered to the segments

- Key resources that describe what is needed to deliver the value propositions

- Key partners that describe suppliers, distributors, and others outside of the company or organization needed to deliver the value propositions

- Cost structure describing the most significant cost items needed to deliver the value propositions and/or respond to threats or potential changes in the future

- Revenue streams describing revenue (or monetary value) produced by the delivered value propositions and pressures that could change the revenue figures

If we revisit our example of a manufacturer of industrial equipment here, we might fill out a business value canvas with the following information:

- Value propositions – Provider of automated manufacturing equipment (requiring fewer operators and enabling improved volume and quality of manufactured goods) and ongoing timely maintenance of such equipment

- Customers – Manufacturers who use such equipment within specific industries to produce goods (e.g., automotive manufacturers)

- Relationships – Key roles within customers including individuals engaged in manufacturing quality control of goods produced, operational excellence, and production

- Channels – Direct and indirect sales, delivery, and support organizations

- Key activities – Research and development of new automated capabilities and robotics, monitoring and predictive analysis of potential equipment failure, and just-in-time dispatching of service personnel and spare parts

- Key resources – Skilled individuals to deliver the key activities and adequate inventories of parts

- Key partners – Suppliers, distributors, and service personnel from third parties

- Cost structure – Costs of labor, inventory, sales, marketing, and transportation as well as additional costs incurred if expectations were not met

- Revenue streams – Obtained from equipment sold, warranties sold, and additional services sold

A word of caution is necessary here, however. Any amount of research that you do before the workshop takes place could cause bias. What you think should be important to the company might not be all that important to key sponsors and other participants in the workshop. You should be prepared to throw away some of your pre-workshop knowledge if the discussion heads in an entirely different direction and/or some of your research is proven to be irrelevant.

Top-of-Mind Industry Topics

We will next look at some of the topics that we have seen are top of mind in a select group of industries today, especially those that often drive software development and AI projects. The industries we will describe here include agribusiness, construction and mining, education and research, finance (banking and portfolio management, insurance), healthcare (payers, providers, and senior living), hospitality, legal firms and professional services, manufacturing (consumer packaged goods, equipment, and vehicles), media and entertainment, oil and gas, pharmaceuticals and medical devices, property management, retail, telecommunications, transportation, and utilities.

Note   You might use some of the following areas of focus present in similar organizations to broaden conversations at the outset of a workshop, especially if the organization that you are working with has unclear goals. You might begin with the observation that "other companies in this industry have said that the following are top of mind" to get creative juices flowing.

Agribusiness

Agribusiness refers to farm-related businesses and agencies including those concerned with optimally growing crops, maintaining livestock, and their delivery to market. Areas of focus that might be explored in a workshop include

- Improving production, quality, and yield including optimized planting, growing, and harvesting of crops and care of livestock

- Minimizing usage of pesticides and/or antibiotics and/or other natural resources such as water

- Supply chain optimization including just-in-time (JIT) delivery of harvested crops and livestock minimizing storage and associated costs and improving quality and time to market

- Improving partnerships between growers, livestock owners, suppliers, and processors

- Improving sales and marketing with delivery of the right products to market at the right time, improving revenue, and reducing surplus

Construction and Mining

Companies involved in the construction of buildings, transportation networks, other infrastructure, and mining might wish to focus a Design Thinking workshop on one or more of these areas:

- Ensuring safety to meet regulations and reducing the need for worker compensation payouts

- Providing optimal crew scheduling and required training

- Optimizing resource planning and utilization of equipment and parts minimizing downtime

- Improving quality of work and on-time delivery of milestones and projects

- Improving win rates and profitability through more accurate bidding for new jobs

Education and Research

Organizations involved in primary-, secondary-, and university-level education and research generally want to focus on one or more of these areas:

- Improving academic performance of students

- Measuring and improving the impact of faculty

- Optimizing the determination of ideal student candidates for admissions

- Measuring utilization of facilities and optimizing their usage and maintenance

- Shortening time to research results and improving research effectiveness and reputation of the organization

- Improving alumni participation and financial support

Finance – Banking and Portfolio Management

Companies involved in banking and/or portfolio management frequently focus Design Thinking workshops on one of these areas:

- Improving customer uptake of products and services across multiple financial offerings

- Understanding and increasing customer interactions and information sharing across devices and physical locations

- Optimizing staffing and physical locations (such as branch bank locations and locations of ATMs)

- Reducing exposure to risk and determining illicit activities faster

- Optimizing performance of financial assets

Finance – Insurance

Insurance companies are faced with traditional concerns and many new challenges as their businesses evolve. Areas of focus often include

- Providing faster payment of legitimate claims to their best customers

- Detecting fraudulent claims sooner

- More accurately pricing offerings based on risk profiles and property utilization and location

- Providing better and faster services through customers' mobile devices (including leveraging images captured by clients on their devices)

- Enabling entry into new business areas such as consulting and specialty products

Healthcare Payers

Healthcare payers share some of the same focus areas as other insurers but also have some unique areas of focus. These include

- Optimizing quality of care with partner healthcare providers to minimize costs of treatments and improve outcomes

- More accurately predicting cost of care for insured groups

- Providing faster payment of legitimate claims

- Detecting fraudulent claims sooner

- Improving services available through customers' mobile devices

- Improving effectiveness of marketing and promotions

Healthcare Providers and Senior Living

Healthcare providers and senior living facilities share some of the same areas of focus as healthcare payers but also have a deeper focus on care giving. These areas include

- Improving quality of care, care planning, and quality of life

- Improving inpatient and in-home patient/guest monitoring

- Optimizing staffing to control costs while maintaining quality

- Improving sharing of information with patients, guests, and families through online/mobile device interactions

- Optimizing utilization of facilities

- Optimizing management of supplies and equipment

Hospitality

The hospitality industry includes management of hotel rooms, bed and breakfast properties, cruise ships, and related properties. Focus areas for Design Thinking workshops sometimes include

- Optimizing room occupation and pricing

- Improving customer service, food, and entertainment offerings

- Providing seamless reservation management across systems and mobile devices

- Improving financial return from customer loyalty programs

- Optimizing staffing

- Optimizing locations and management of facilities and supplies

Legal Firms and Professional Services

Legal firms and other professional services firms (such as consulting companies) share similar business focus areas, and these frequently are explored during Design Thinking workshops. These areas include

- Enabling faster discovery of past similar cases/engagements

- Providing better analysis of engagements to predict likelihood of successful outcomes

- Improving practice management including tracking of time and expenses

- Uncovering demand for new services that can grow the firm

- Optimizing staffing and skills based on current and projected future demand

Manufacturing – Consumer Packaged Goods

Consumer packaged goods (CPG) manufacturers often focus Design Thinking workshops on one or more of the following business areas:

- Improving methods to understand changing consumer preferences

- Improving brand awareness (through promotions, advertising, and product placement) and the value of brands

- Exploring new ways of going to market and delivery of goods

- Optimizing product production and supply chain based on historic information and projected demand

- Ensuring product quality while maintaining/improving margins

- Improving consumer satisfaction in call center interactions

Manufacturing – Equipment and Vehicles

Manufacturers of equipment used in industrial settings (such as equipment sold to manufacturers of vehicles, mechanical parts, electronics components, etc.) and in business settings have a variety of areas they might want to focus upon including

- Improving product mix based on changing customers' requirements

- Adding support offerings and reducing support costs and warranty funding through improved product quality and predictive maintenance

- Improving safety related to the usage of products (e.g., through increased automation)

- Optimizing customers' production output

- Ensuring just-in-time delivery of parts and components in the supply chain

Media and Entertainment

Media and entertainment companies include streaming services, television networks, cable providers, theme parks, and sports and theater venues. Some of the focus areas for these companies include

- Enabling differentiated content creation, acquisition, and management

- Maximizing advertising effectiveness, revenue, and improving ordering/ticketing across offerings

- Improving service reputation (ease of self-service, installation and repair scheduling, complaint handling)

- Growing and developing offerings in non-traditional channels

- Enabling venue management excellence and revenue optimization through optimized traffic flows and seating options and better targeted concessions

Oil and Gas

Companies in this industry are focused on the exploration, delivery, and processing of oil and gas. Topics for discussion during Design Thinking workshops typically include discussing one or more of the following:

- Improving exploration results through more insightful and timely analysis of geologic data

- Enabling optimal maintenance of upstream, mid-stream, and downstream equipment

- Optimizing supply chains and human resources

- Improving management of environmental risk and safety

- Maximizing value of real estate owned and under consideration for purchase

- Improving public and regulator perception

Pharmaceuticals and Medical Devices

For pharmaceutical companies and medical device manufacturers, these are some of the focus areas that might be explored in Design Thinking workshops:

- Enabling faster clinical trials (proving success or failing sooner at lower cost during research)

- Understanding effectiveness of drugs/devices as patients utilize them and identifying emerging risks sooner

- Determining counterfeiting of drugs or devices sooner

- Predicting demand for drugs/devices and determining promotion effectiveness

- Improving management of sales and distribution

Property Management

Companies and government agencies that manage properties will frequently focus on one or more of these areas:

- Improving their property portfolio to match current and projected future demand

- Improving their assessment of the true value of properties

- Gaining a better understanding of changing demographics (and its future impact on the value of properties)

- Reducing investments considered higher risk

- Improving their understanding of the causes and locations of vacancies

Retail

Retailers face many challenges as shopper preferences continue to change at ever faster rates. Among the areas frequently focused upon in Design Thinking workshops are

- Improving omni-channel (seamless multi-channel) experiences

- Improving store operations including merchandise layout, reducing merchandise loss, and providing optimal staffing

- Determining optimal retail and distribution locations and providing better management of real estate

- Improving merchandise and category management

- Improving advertising effectiveness across all channels

Telecommunications

Telecommunications companies provide networks for data centers, mobile devices, and landlines. Companies that provide such services often focus on the following areas in workshops:

- Improving customer acquisition (including promotions optimization)

- Creating new and differentiated offerings

- Maintaining and improving network quality of service and security

- Predicting unusual events (e.g., weather) and managing repairs

- Optimizing their supply chain, equipment, and staff

- Improving worker safety

Transportation

Companies and government agencies managing transportation equipment and networks often have one or more of the following areas as top of mind:

- Optimizing routing of equipment and operators to match passenger and/or freight demands, meet schedules, and mitigate costs

- Improving availability of needed equipment through predictive maintenance

- Reducing traffic congestion whenever possible

- Optimizing supply chain for just-in-time availability of replacement parts and supplies

- Improving safety consistent with existing and emerging regulations

- Modifying customer loyalty programs to increase revenue and reduce churn

- Improving right-of-way maintenance and management

Utilities

Public utilities deliver electricity, gas, and water to businesses and homes. Areas of discussion in Design Thinking workshops might include

- Managing demand by offering incentives and other proactive measures

- Maximizing utility availability through improved preventive maintenance

- Optimizing their supply chain, equipment, and staffing

- Maintaining service during unusual weather and other environmental events

- Meeting more stringent regulatory and environmental requirements

- Improving worker and facility safety

- Improving management of right-of-way and real estate locations

Workshop Facility and Supplies

We have taken part in Design Thinking workshops that have a wide variation in the number of participants, ranging from a half dozen to several dozen. Having a single room that comfortably holds everyone is necessary (even if it is planned to send teams into separate rooms for some of the exercises). This is because all participants should see the problems and solutions that each team is working on so that they can evaluate them, provide feedback, and spark new ideas.

Utilizing conference rooms off-site from the company or organization is preferable when seeking to avoid physical interruptions caused by normal day-to-day activities.

Meeting rooms should have ample whiteboard and wall space to display the results of exercises. Ideally, food and refreshments should be provided in adjacent space to maximize the time spent in the workshop.

Figure 2-2 shows a typical conference room used in a Design Thinking workshop.

Figure 2-2. *Conference room used in a Design Thinking workshop*

The facilitator is typically responsible for providing the following supplies (or arranging to have them present within the workshop facility):

- Sticky note easel pad(s) and easel(s) – One per team taking part.

- Multi-color small sticky notes – Supply each participant with multiple colors (colors usage is described in later chapters covering workshop exercises).

- Writing markers – Supply each participant with a marker such that when they write their ideas, the markings will be readable from a distance.

- Stickers such as stars and smiley faces – Used by each participant when voting occurs during the workshop.

- Index cards – Multiple cards are provided to each participant.

- Plain sheets of paper (8x10) – A few sheets are provided to each participant.

- Squeezable toys – Enough toys should be on the table such that each participant can have at least one (as these can help spur creative ideas).

- Name tents – To identify each participant.

- Timing clock(s) – Visible to each participant during timed exercises.

- Mobile camera – Usually a mobile phone, this is used to capture output from exercises.

A typical set of materials for each participant appears in Figure 2-3.

Figure 2-3. *Typical set of participant materials in a Design Thinking workshop*

The supplies that we described are normally available in office supply stores if not already stocked in the company or organization where the workshop will take place. Dollar discount stores are a great and inexpensive source for the squeezable toys.

Online brainstorming applications are sometimes considered as an alternative to physical sticky notes and whiteboards. These can simplify the bill of materials needed and might be considered useful when participants are (less optimally) widely dispersed. However, some instruction is usually needed on how to use the tools and some of the spontaneity of writing ideas on sticky notes and then collaborating on where to place the notes on whiteboards and easels is lost. So, experienced facilitators often shy away from using such applications (though technology people frequently will like the idea of this approach) while also mandating that all workshop participants be at the same location.

Summary

Proper preparation for a Design Thinking workshop builds a foundation for later success. Failure to do so will likely result in less than optimal workshop results. You should now understand how to do the following:

- Describe what the Design Thinking workshop is to others.

- Define the key roles of participants who should take part in the workshop and their responsibilities.

- Set expectations regarding coordination needed between the facilitator and sponsor(s) prior to the workshop.

- Important rules and guidelines that should be put in place during the workshop.

- Understand how to perform independent research the state of the business.

- Leverage what could be top of mind among participants in a variety of industries.

- Obtain the proper facility and the necessary supplies for a workshop.

Next, in Chapter 3, we start exploring methods and tools used in exploring the problem space during a typical workshop. We will show how our participants who take part in these exercises can define a problem that they will want to solve.

CHAPTER 3

Problem Definition

When some organizations begin taking part in a Design Thinking workshop, all participants in the workshop are laser-focused on ideating around a single goal. In other organizations, the participants might come to the workshop having ill-defined or multiple goals in mind. In this chapter, we describe the best practices involved in figuring out a goal for each team to focus upon and scoping out an agreed-upon problem to be solved.

We will traverse the problem space diamond that we introduced in the Double Diamond approach described in Chapter 1. After we come to agreement around a goal, we will broaden our exploration of the problem and then narrow our focus to single problem that must be solved. Included in the exercises that we cover in this chapter are approaches to gaining a deeper understanding of the stakeholders that care about the problem and defining the potential benefits, emerging new opportunities and challenges that the organization might encounter if they choose to solve it.

This chapter provides important guidance for facilitators of these workshops, but it is also written to provide insight for other participants into the methods and tools employed. For example, key stakeholders can gain an understanding of how this workshop provides an approach that helps them more clearly understand the problems that are most important. Such stakeholders should also begin to gain an appreciation of how the workshop will help them gain buy-in from its participants.

Participants should take away that while solutioning does not begin until they traverse the solution space diamond that is focused upon in Chapter 4, they can gain a more comprehensive understanding of the problem to be solved using the approach that we describe in this chapter. In fact, in our experience, problem definition often takes more time than solutioning in these workshops.

Most adults find that staying focused in fully understanding a problem is very challenging because they are tempted to want to hurry up and solve it. However, the patience to explore problems in detail by becoming a good investigator will uncover more details that are relevant in determining a higher-quality solution.

© Robert Stackowiak and Tracey Kelly 2020
R. Stackowiak and T. Kelly, *Design Thinking in Software and AI Projects*

Elisabeth McClure, in a TED talk titled "Are Children Really More Creative Than Adults," stated that research shows children spend more time in divergent thinking (e.g., looking at possibilities and expanding options of what is or could be) but not appropriateness. So, they have more cognitive flexibility than adults.

According to McClure, adults like to spend more time in convergent thinking using critical thinking to decide what to do. It is harder for adults to spend time in divergent thinking. However, the success of this workshop depends on creativity that is a balance of originality and appropriateness. Thus, facilitators need to work hard to keep parts of the workshop from being frustrating for many adults.

This chapter provides guidance, methods, and tools on how to do this and contains the following major sections:

- Self-introductions and workshop overview

- Selecting goals and diverse teams

- Creating a unified vision and scope

- Mapping stakeholders and personas

- Positives, opportunities, and negatives

- Refine to one problem statement

- Summary

Self-Introductions and Workshop Overview

The morning of the workshop, the facilitator should arrive early to make sure that the facility, materials, and any food to be provided are set up and ready. Participants' nameplates are sometimes distributed to assigned seats, but they might also remain in a cluster on the table such that participants can initially choose their own seats. Keep in mind that participants will move to other room locations anyways once they become part of a team.

To establish the precedence that the workshop will be carefully timed, the day should begin at the time that was agreed upon during pre-workshop preparation. Workshops typically begin between 8:30 and 9:30 a.m. Upon the arrival and seating of participants, the facilitator will explain the layout of the facility including the locations of restrooms, emergency exits, and food. Some discussion about when breaks might occur during the day and an explanation of the purpose of the toys present on the table(s) also occurs.

At this point, it is also a good idea for everyone to be reminded of the agreed-upon rules for the day that we introduced in Chapter 2. The facilitator should reiterate the following:

- Bring an open mindset to the workshop.

- Be physically present during the workshop.

- Laptops will be turned off and other mobile devices put away (if these are not being used only for taking notes) – no email or texting unrelated to the workshop should be exchanged when it takes place.

- Exercises will be timed to keep the workshop on track.

- Any discussions determined out of scope during the workshop will be noted and deferred to an appropriate time.

In order to bring an open mindset, participants should be reminded that they will need to guard against their own biases. Potential biases that need to be avoided can be classified as follows:

- Recency bias – A tendency to overvalue the most recent information

- Anchor bias – Relying too much on pre-existing or initial information

- Bandwagon bias – A tendency to agree to maintain harmony in a group to the extent of not reaching a better decision or idea

The facilitator should help maintain focus on the exercises during the workshop by making sure that everyone is physically and mentally present (hence the closing of laptops and elimination of non-essential emails and messaging). The timing of exercises will also help keep focus on the tasks at hand.

The facilitator should be cognizant of signs of covert and overt resistance that might be present in some participants. Covert resistance is often expressed in negative body language, such as participants having crossed arms, pointing their index fingers, making sideways glances, gripping the table with their hands, biting fingernails and pencils, crossing legs, and kicking or fidgeting. More overt signs might include lack of participation and input during team activities.

Facilitators and proctors can often pull such individuals back into participating in the exercises and activities by prompting them for input. Facilitators and proctors might also suggest that they should serve as a spokesperson by presenting the output from the current exercise that the team is working on.

Note   Brainteasers are sometimes used by the facilitator here and/or during other periods within the workshop if the participants seem to be less than enthusiastic during certain exercises or dialogues. These can generate a lot of additional energy, especially when participants are highly competitive with each other, and encourage out-of-the-box thinking. Typical examples of brainteasers include exercises that involve participants competing to solve visual and physical puzzles.

Tool: ELMO Card

A tool that can be introduced at this time and used throughout the entire workshop is the ELMO card. These cards are useful for when discussions become too protracted and need to be deferred.

Discussions that become extended and that begin to explore out-of-scope areas that are not relevant to the workshop can result in frustration among participants. As frustration grows, it is important that each participant feels empowered to suggest setting aside the discussion. In anticipation such situations, the facilitator might ask participants to write "ELMO" on an index card during this point in the workshop. The letters stand for "Enough, Let's Move On." This method for group focus enablement was introduced by Laurie Edwards Gray, a customer experience consultant in Atlanta.

If anyone feels that the workshop is getting derailed by a discussion, they simply hold up or throw their ELMO card during the workshop. (Laurie recommends that the facilitator gently throw the first ELMO card to break the ice and show "safe" usage. Chances are that several participants, upon seeing the first card, will do the same. If they do not, the discussion should continue.) The facilitator will make note of the discussion on a whiteboard, and it will be addressed at the end of the workshop to either schedule another time to discuss and escalate or any other action the room deems relevant to the topic.

Method: Introduction Card

This method or activity is focused on getting everyone involved in interactions as team exercises are critical to the success of the workshop. It is very possible, given the diverse roles of the participants, that not everyone will know each other in the room. So, this activity gets everyone involved by having each person create their own "baseball card" on an index card.

Participants begin by simply drawing a stick figure representing themselves (to get them comfortable with drawing, since drawing occurs at various points in the workshop). The facilitator, proctor(s), and scribe(s) also typically take part in this exercise and prepare their own cards. Each person also lists some basic information on the card including their name, title/role, and hobbies.

The facilitator gives everyone 5 or 10 minutes to prepare the card. When time is up, each participant then individually shows their card and introduces themselves (thus gaining comfort in presenting to the group).

Figure 3-1 illustrates a typical card prepared by one of this book's authors. Here, the author provides the nickname they are using in the workshop (preferring to be called "Bob" instead of "Robert"), roles in the workshop (facilitator and architect), and a couple of personal hobbies (baseball fan and wine collector).

Figure 3-1. *Sample workshop card describing one of this book's authors*

A variation sometimes used in providing participants' introductions is to have each individual participant partner with another person. Each participant interviews their partner. They then draw and label a card that describes their partner with a stick figure and similar information to that previously described (name, title/role, hobbies). Finally, each person introduces their partner to the group.

Method: Participant Connections

At this point, the person or their partner can be prompted to write the name and role of the person just introduced on a whiteboard. People in similar roles in the same organization are typically grouped together. Lines are then drawn to persons in different groups, and relationships are denoted among the various groups on the drawing. Such a diagram further helps to explain how the person fits in the organization.

Figure 3-2 illustrates some of the workshop participants in our supply chain optimization example and their connections. We see how the plant workers are related to IT and the data science team. The identified plant workers are users of and supported by IT. Plant workers are users of solutions developed by the data science team. The data science team helps drive specifications for the infrastructure that IT provides.

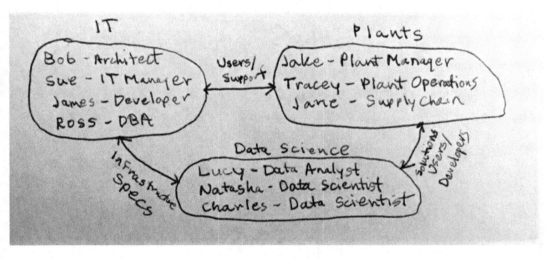

Figure 3-2. *Workshop participants and their connections*

The facilitator then provides an overview of Design Thinking and how it will be applied during the workshop. Typical topics covered here (and previously introduced in Chapter 1 of this book) include

- A brief history of Design Thinking

- The intersection of innovation and design

- How Design Thinking can mitigate costs of change

- How bias can influence design

- The Double Diamond approach including discovery and definition in the problem space and design and delivery in the solution space

This introduction to Design Thinking gives the participants a common basic understanding as to the methodology. It also serves as a road map and explanation of the agenda that will be followed in the workshop.

Selecting Goals and Diverse Teams

We are now ready to discuss the goal or goals to be further defined as problems to be solved in this portion of the workshop. In our experience, when organizations come into the workshop with a single goal in mind, it is usually driven by the sponsoring stakeholder. However, it is also common for stakeholders and other participants to come to the workshop with multiple potential goals in mind, and it is also possible that they might be unsure of what goals are important to the organization.

We'll next discuss methods for setting goals and then describe creating diverse teams that will be in place throughout the workshop.

Method: How Might We

If the situation is one where multiple goals are being discussed, the participants should decide if they want to tackle them all or narrow them down. An exercise to narrow them down begins with each participant in the room writing the goals that they think are top of mind for their organization on sticky notes and placing them on a whiteboard. If the facilitator sees that several of the sticky notes state the same goal, they will group these together.

Note   The facilitator should not provide insights or ideas during this exercise and other exercises that we will describe. Instead, the facilitator should help the participants in the room discover them on their own. The facilitator should also frame each exercise prior to it beginning (including the time allocated) and provide guidance and reassurance while directing participants away from premature consideration of solutions.

The participants are next asked to use one of the stickers that they have been provided to vote on the goal that they think is most important. The facilitator tallies the goal (or goals) with the most votes. A goal or goals with the most votes are then put into the form of "how might we" statements. The writing down of goals and voting exercise should take about 10 minutes.

Using our example of a manufacturer of industrial equipment introduced in Chapter 2, we might choose the goal of optimizing the supply chain. So, a statement the participants could come up with is "How might we optimize our supply chain?" If other goals are going to be addressed by certain teams, "how might we" statements would also be written for those.

The statement(s) are then written on a sticky easel sheet that would be posted in the common meeting room so that all would see it/them throughout the workshop. That is illustrated in Figure 3-3.

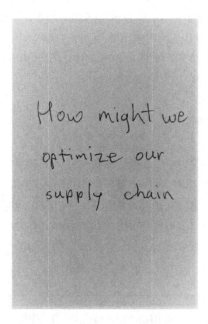

Figure 3-3. *Goal statement in our example*

We are now ready to select the workshop teams. Typical team sizes are four to eight people. If multiple goals are to be addressed during the workshop, each team should have a line-of-business leader particularly interested in solving the specific team goal. (If multiple teams are addressing the same goal, those team leaders should have an interest in reaching that common goal.)

Method: Team Naming

Naming your team or teams is a good method to employ when you want to create unity, excitement, and ownership of outcomes within a team. Having teams name themselves is also an activity that can serve as an icebreaker and help people who don't know each other to actually begin to come together as a team.

Team leaders should make sure that their team contains individuals in diverse roles who will be impacted by reaching the goal. These individuals might include line-of-business representatives (leaders and frontline workers), business analysts/ data scientists, partners/customers, support teams, and IT software developers and managers. This diversity will help to ensure more complete discussions and expressions of varying points of view during problem discovery and definition. It should also lead to better solution design and delivery discussions later.

Each team then gathers in a designated area within the conference room (or to separate rooms if pre-arranged) around easels that have sticky sheets. Each will agree upon a name for their team, write it on a sheet of sticky easel paper, and then also draw a simple picture related to the team name and the team's goal. The team selection and naming should take about 10 minutes.

Figure 3-4 illustrates an example coming from a team working on the supply chain optimization problem. They've drawn a picture using arrows to represent supplies coming into a manufacturing plant and output leaving. They've named their team the "Right Time/Right Place Team." In this example, their goal is reflected in their name: to get the right supplies and output to the right place at the right time.

Figure 3-4. *Sample team drawing and name*

All teams then gather into a single room (if not already in a common room). A spokesperson for each team explains their artwork and team name to the other teams in the main conference room. Participants on other teams can ask for clarification as each team is presented. Teams might modify their artwork as needed based upon feedback and then post the drawing onto designated wall space (where they will subsequently post other exercise renderings).

Method: Abstraction Ladder

Use this method when you are trying to help the team gain greater alignment and unify all their goals and objectives. They can gain a clearer unified vision of a goal through the abstraction ladder exercise.

Team members gather again into their separate groups around their easels. Each team begins by writing their "how might we" statement from earlier across the center of an easel sticky sheet. Above the statement, they draw an arrow pointed up along with the word "why." This is where the team will describe why they might take this action (the "so what" reasons). Below the statement, they draw an arrow pointed down along with the word "how." This is where they will begin to describe how they will take this action.

Next, each of the team participants writes as many "why" and "how" statements related to the goal that they can think of on their sticky notes. They post them on the easel sticky sheets getting broader with "why" statements as they move up the sheet and narrower with their "how" statements as they move down. (Facilitators, proctors, and/ or team leaders typically help with grouping overlapping notes and placing them on the sheet.) This part of the exercise takes about 10 minutes.

In our imaginary supply chain optimization example, the team came up with narrow "why" statements that include "meet production demand," "eliminate waste," and "improve partnerships." Broader "why" statements that they came up with include "gain market share" and "improve margins."

Broad "how" example statements include "improve tracking" and "improve quality." The notion of "improve tracking" was narrowed down by the team into "understand shortages," "view key metrics," and "alert plant" and "alert supplier." "Improve quality" was narrowed into "standardize processes."

Figure 3-5 illustrates what a typical easel sticky sheet might look like at this stage in our supply chain optimization example after team participants have placed their "why" and "how" sticky notes and they have been sorted from broad to narrow.

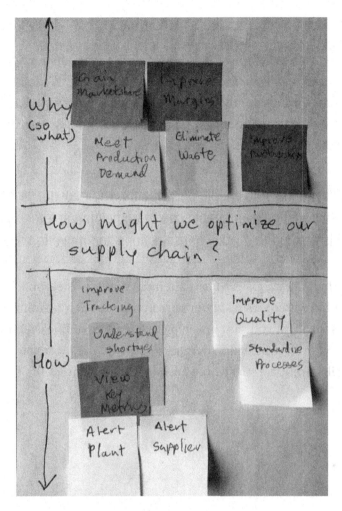

Figure 3-5. *Sample unified vision easel sticky sheet with "whys" and "hows"*

Note   The supply chain optimization example presented throughout this chapter and Chapter 4 is an imaginary example and is not representative of any past single client that the authors worked with. It is meant to portray a theoretical set of exercise results in an area of popular interest we have seen driving Design Thinking workshops in certain industries. You will find that any workshop that you take part in will yield its own unique set of problems and outcomes linked to current business processes and the needs of key stakeholders and their organization.

Tool: Voting

We now have a variety of "why" and "how" statements on the abstraction ladder, any one of which could be used to narrow the scope of the effort ahead. A tool that can be used in different situations throughout the entire workshop to narrow choices is voting. This is typically accomplished by using stickers (i.e., using dot, smiley face, or star stickers to mark preferences or vote on topics).

Note   The goal of voting is to enable participants who may not be comfortable debating to select a mutually agreeable choice and eliminate other choices. It's helpful to use this method to quickly get selections and move forward.

Each team participant chooses a best statement that is posted on the abstraction ladder easel by voting with one sticker per person over about a 10-minute period. The statement that has the most votes is chosen by that team to define their initial scope.

In our example, "meet production demand" received the most votes as it has the most stickers. We illustrate the sticky note and stickers in Figure 3-6.

Figure 3-6. *Example "best statement" shown after vote with stickers attached*

Each team then has a spokesperson present their entire diagram to the other teams and describe why they selected the winning statement. If different goals are being pursued among teams, each team solicits feedback and possibly further refines their scope. If a single goal is being pursued by all the teams, another vote takes place and a single scope statement is selected for all the teams to subsequently work from.

Mapping Stakeholders and Personas

Projects require a commitment of money and other resources. At some point along the way, the importance of solving the problem that you identify must be supported by key stakeholders. These stakeholders might include sponsors and decision-makers, gatekeepers and approvers, and important influencers (including frontline workers coming face to face with the problem in their day-to-day activities). In these exercises, we begin to identify and characterize some of these key individuals.

Method: Stakeholder Mapping

Within each team, individual team members begin by writing the names of stakeholders and the stakeholders' roles or titles on sticky notes. They bring them forward and post them on a sticky easel sheet. A team leader or proctor eliminates duplicates and clusters the stakeholders into groups. A circle is then drawn around each group and they are labeled.

In our supply chain optimization example, the team identified stakeholders in the following groups: C-level, logistics and transportation, plant operations, suppliers, sales and marketing, and IT. C-level stakeholders in this example include the CEO, CFO, and CIO. Logistics and transportation stakeholders include logistics management and logistics analysts. Plant operations stakeholders include plant operations management and plant operations workers. Suppliers are represented by a single set of stakeholders in the example. Sales and marketing stakeholders include representatives from each organization. IT stakeholders include individuals involved in data management, data science, software development, and IT infrastructure.

Lines are then drawn connecting the groups that represent their relationships to each other, and the nature of the relationships is appropriately denoted as labels on the lines. Some of the relationships in our supply chain example include demand generated by sales and marketing for products produced from plant operations, exchanges of data facilitated by IT, and exchanges of pipeline information with the C-level. Logistics and transportation coordinates with plant operations and suppliers and interacts with IT through the exchange of data.

Figure 3-7 illustrates a stakeholder map consistent with our supply chain optimization example.

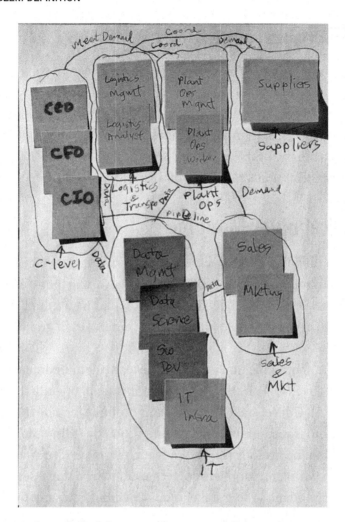

Figure 3-7. *Example stakeholder map denoting relationships*

After preparation of the stakeholder map (usually taking about 10 to 15 minutes to do this), designated spokespersons from each team describe their stakeholder map to other teams and solicit comments. Additional stakeholders and/or relationships might be added as a result of these comments. The diagrams are posted on the wall space assigned to each team.

Method: Proto-Personas

Each team then chooses two or three key stakeholders to focus upon that influence, impact, or control the scope of the problem to be solved.

A sticky easel sheet is prepared to represent each stakeholder group is identified as a proto-persona by first dividing each sheet into four quadrants. The quadrants are filled in as follows:

- Stakeholder name and demographic information (such as title/role)

- Stakeholder behaviors and tasks, especially those related to the selected problem scope (you can use the "jobs to be done" method also described in this section to further hone into the tasks that matter to this proto-persona)

- Stakeholder needs, goals, and motivations

- Stakeholder frustrations and challenges

Note   Proto-personas are based on opinion and observation from other parties. They can contain some bias and should be validated through additional research of the actual group. But they are a good place to begin understanding the needs, motivations, and tasks of others. For example, you might define user experience personas to represent that group of stakeholders in order to build empathy for them. In comparison, high-fidelity personas are typically created from research, interviews, observations, and facts.

About 30 minutes should be allocated for each team to prepare their easel sticky sheets (so, about 10 to 15 minutes for each stakeholder). The sheets are then posted on the wall space assigned to each team. Stakeholder descriptions are explained to the other teams by an assigned team spokesperson. Other teams can then provide comments and suggest adjustments where needed.

A key stakeholder in our supply chain optimization example is the plant manager. Their behaviors and tasks include coordination of plant teams, monitoring production, supplies and quality of goods produced, and reporting plant and production status to senior management. Their needs, goals, and motivations include reducing waste, improving quality, and meeting production goals set by management. Frustrations and challenges include frequent oversupply and undersupply of materials, inaccurate forecasts of sales, and a lack of quality metrics. Figure 3-8 shows how these items might appear when written out into quadrants on a flip-chart page.

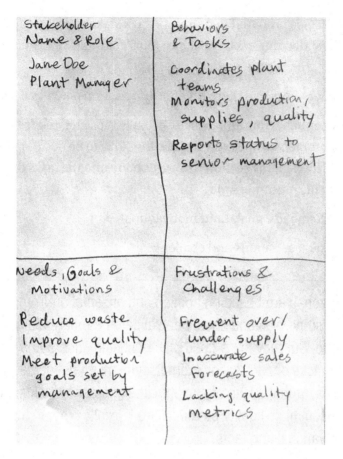

Figure 3-8. *Example stakeholder description for a plant manager*

In addition to this format, you might want to build "jobs to be done" statements for the stakeholder. The format of this statement is "When (a situation occurs) the stakeholder wants to (take action) so they can (expected outcome)". What follows is an example for a stakeholder that is a plant manager:

> *When undersupply occurs, I want to automatically alert supplier so I can minimize production disruption.*

And Figure 3-9 shows how the statement might be written on a flip-chart page. Notice in Figure 3-9 how key phrases are underlined to highlight what the plant manager is truly concerned about.

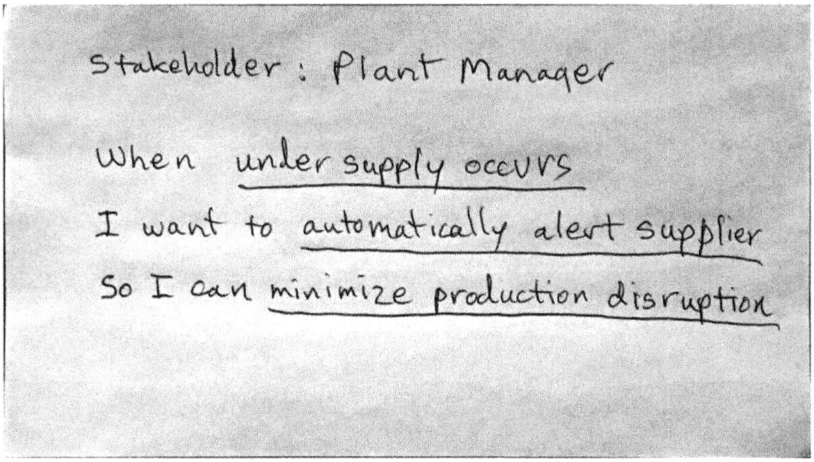

Figure 3-9. Example "jobs to be done" statement for the plant manager

Additional sheets describing other stakeholders can provide the teams with additional perspectives regarding the importance of solving the problem that they are thinking about pursuing.

In our example, the C-level leaders have a more complete view of running the business. Their behaviors and tasks include setting strategy, managing investments, determining margins, forecasting sales and financial results, optimizing their business, and building the company's reputation. Their needs, goals, and motivations include more accurate forecasts, smarter investments, increased margins, and decreased risk. Frustrations and challenges include a lack of timely data, aging facilities, widely varying manufacturing equipment sophistication and age, widely varying skills among employees, and varying performance among their plants.

Figure 3-10 shows a flip-chart page for C-Suite stakeholders. The upper left quadrant identifies the stakeholder as being the C-Suite people such as the CEO, CFO, and CIO. The remaining quadrants in clockwise order list behavioral tasks, frustrations and challenges, and finally needs, goals, and motivations.

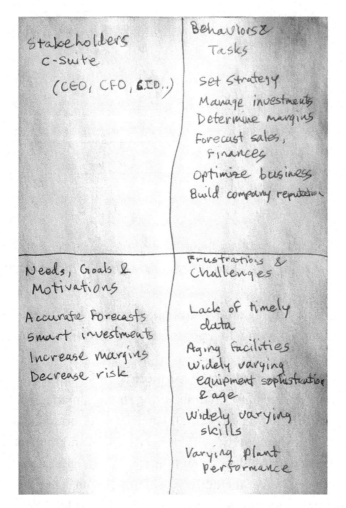

Figure 3-10. *Example stakeholder description for the C-level leadership*

Positives, Opportunities, and Negatives

In this exercise, we identify positive situations that will occur as a result of addressing the scope that was previously identified, new opportunities that could emerge, and negative situations that will also likely occur. We have seen this popular exercise represented in drawings on easel sheets as a rose (with rose, bud, and thorn), as a sailboat (with sails, wind, and anchors), and as a stoplight (green light, yellow light, and red light). We then cluster our sticky notes into areas of impact.

We begin by describing the rose-bud-thorn method here.

Method: Rose-Bud-Thorn

Each person within each team uses sticky notes to indicate what should work well, new opportunities, and likely problems that will be encountered in addressing the scope. Each person writes positive statements as it relates to the scope they are addressing on pink sticky notes, considered to be rose items. Opportunities with potential are written on green sticky notes, considered to be buds. Negative statements or challenges are written on blue sticky notes and are considered as thorns. By denoting these types of statements on different colored sticky notes, it will make identifying the category that they fit into easier when each team member places their sticky notes onto a sticky easel sheet.

Note   The purpose of this exercise is to help everyone clearly see the pros and cons of addressing the identified scope. At this point, the facilitator can also ask what the cost is if nothing is done, because asking about cost helps to create a sense of urgency around the change that needs to happen. This method also uncovers problems that need to be avoided in the design ideas that the teams will generate later.

In our supply chain optimization example, team members denoted that positive outcomes include "improve sales," "improve revenue," "improve finance forecasts," and "understand shortages sooner." Opportunities that they identified include "quality improvement," "improve marketing outcomes," "reduce waste," "new data sources," and "proactive fixing." Negative implications identified include "project cost," "data quality issues," "manufacturing equipment upgrades," and "union contract implications."

Figure 3-11 illustrates these sticky notes placed appropriately on a rose-bud-thorn illustration. Positive outcomes are placed in the upper right next to the rose, opportunities are placed in the middle left next to the bud, and negative implications are placed in the lower right next to the thorns.

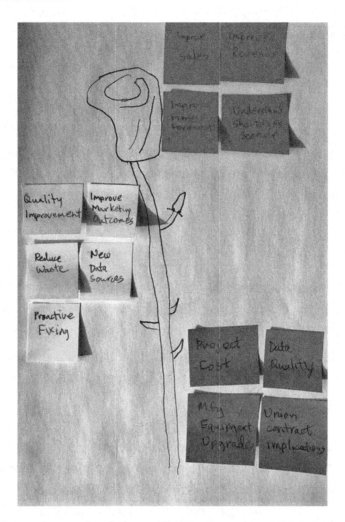

Figure 3-11. *Example rose-bud-thorn illustration of positives, opportunities, and negatives*

Method: Clustering Areas of Impact

The team leader and/or proctor then places the sticky notes into clusters on a different easel sticky sheet into areas of impact. The clusters are labeled appropriately (with input from team members).

Taking our rose-bud-thorn sticky notes from our example, the team chose to group them into areas of impact as illustrated in Figure 3-12. These areas included concerns at the C-level, improving plant operations, managing and providing needed data sources and related IT technology, and improving sales and marketing execution. By using a consistent color scheme for the sticky notes in this exercise, we can now easily pick out positives, opportunities, and negatives impacting each area.

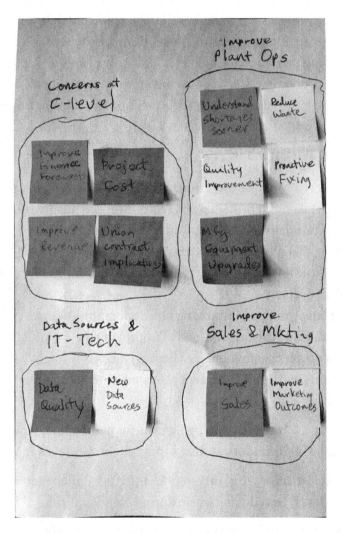

Figure 3-12. *Positives, opportunities, and negatives grouped into areas of impact*

The entire exercise using these two methods should take about 20 to 30 minutes. Upon completion, the sticky easel sheet is placed on the team's wall space. A designated spokesperson from each team describes the positives, negatives, and opportunities to the other teams present and solicits their input.

Refine to One Problem Statement

We now have a variety of possible problems to solve represented by the various clusters. In our example, these include addressing the concerns at the C-level, improving plant operations, addressing data source challenges, and improving sales and marketing efficiencies and outcomes. In order to help converge on the right problem to solve, we can use the "how might we" method to enable focus on the most important challenge.

Method: How Might We…

Each team now selects a "best" single problem category. The category selected is usually most aligned to key stakeholders' needs and has impressive positive outcomes and potential new opportunities with fewer negative implications. Often, team members vote with stickers to make this selection. Once the selection is made, a problem statement is created that states "how might we" do a certain action "for" a primary stakeholder "so that" a desired effect occurs.

In our supply chain example, improving plant operations to meet production demand will be enabled by the original goal of improving the supply chain. So, the team now creates a problem statement that begins with "How might we improve plant operations." Variations of the full statement provided by team members could include statements, such as

- How might we improve plant operations for plant management (or for the C-level) by understanding supply chain shortages sooner

- How might we improve plant operations for plant management (or for the C-level) by reducing waste during manufacturing

- How might we improve plant operations for plant management by improving quality of manufacturing output

- How might we improve plant operations for plant management (or for frontline plant workers) by proactively fixing equipment

- How might we improve plant operations for plant management by upgrading existing equipment

The team then selects (usually by voting) the problem statement it wishes to address. The statement is written on a sticky easel sheet, posted, and explained by a designated team spokesperson to the other teams. Other teams can provide further input. At this point, we have spent about 20 to 30 minutes on this exercise.

If each team is working on a different problem and if the statement is agreed upon, they are ready to move onto design and delivery in the solution space. If multiple teams are working on a single problem, each team will present their statement and another vote will take place such that a single problem statement will be selected as the basis for further exercises.

For our supply chain example, a statement was chosen, and it appears on the sticky easel sheet illustrated in Figure 3-13. The problem statement in the figure reads as follows: "How might we improve plant operations for plant management by understanding supply chain shortages earlier."

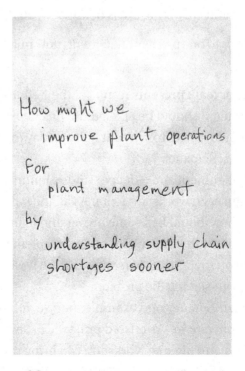

Figure 3-13. *Example problem statement*

Summary

In this chapter, we walked through the first portion of the Design Thinking workshop. We began with self-introductions and a workshop overview. Then we described exercises related to the following problem discovery and definition phases in the problem space diamond of the Double Diamond approach. The individual and team preparation timing for each of these is as follows:

- Introductory individual baseball-style cards – 5 minutes

- Selection of goal(s) – 10 minutes

- Selection of diverse teams and naming – 10 minutes

- Creating a unified vision and scope – 10 minutes

- Identifying and mapping stakeholders – 10 to 15 minutes

- Creating proto-personas of key stakeholders – 30 minutes

- Denoting positives, negatives, and opportunities (rose, bud, and thorn or similar) and clustering areas of impact – 20 to 30 minutes

- Refining our efforts to one problem statement (how might we) – 20 to 30 minutes

When each individual or team presents results of their efforts or votes, about 5 to 10 minutes per individual/team should be allocated. Thus, the length of time for this portion of the workshop could range from about half of a day to a full day depending on the number of teams and participants.

There should now be alignment and a deeper understanding of the nature of the problem to be solved within each workshop team. As all the participants are engaging in the workshop process, they should feel some ownership in finding a solution. All should also understand how addressing the identified problem could be received by key stakeholders based on their proto-personas and the positives, negatives, and opportunities associated with solving the problem.

Using the workshop methodology and example that we outlined thus far, you might be starting to wonder if a software- or AI-related project will always be the result of these exercises. Sometimes, a Design Thinking workshop can bring non-software-related projects to top of mind, especially as we traverse the exercises in the solution space diamond of the Double Diamond approach in the next portion of the workshop.

However, we now have agreement on what is believed to be a real problem. Usually after the problem statement has been selected, the facilitator will call for a break appropriate for the time of day at which this point is reached (e.g., lunch, afternoon refreshments, or conclusion of the first day) since we have now completed the problem space diamond.

In Chapter 4, as we explore ideas related to solving the problem, we will see how software and AI projects frequently do emerge as possible solution outcomes of the workshop.

CHAPTER 4

Solution Definition

The participants and teams who are taking part in the Design Thinking workshop should now be focused on specific problem statements. They have reached the midpoint of the workshop and have experienced divergent and convergent thinking in exploring the problem space.

In this chapter, we describe best practices in using divergent and convergent thinking to determine the best solutions for their problem statements. We will traverse the right-hand solution space diamond of the Double Diamond approach that was introduced in Chapter 1.

Since we have agreement around the problem statement(s), we will broaden our exploration of possible solutions. Then we will narrow our focus to a best solution that has significant desirable business impact and requires an acceptable (and possibly minimal) amount of effort. In this chapter, we describe approaches to help the workshop participants generate many thoughtful ideas for solutions, visualize them, iterate to improve them, and then narrow down to solutions that they want to pursue. We will then build a road map to create ownership and accountability to begin moving solutions from ideas to reality.

Solutioning does not begin until participants fully traverse the left-hand problem space diamond as was described in Chapter 3. Unfortunately, in our experience, participants often want to jump straight to solutioning at the expense of not knowing all the facts, gathering contributing or dependent information, or understanding how change could affect other stakeholders. The prior exercises should have helped participants uncover those areas and should enable them to consider more facts related to the ideas and solutions that they develop in this part of the workshop.

Thus, this chapter contains the following major sections:

- Refresher and restate the challenge

- Getting inspiration

69

R. Stackowiak and T. Kelly, *Design Thinking in Software and AI Projects*

- Understanding innovation ambition

- Solution ideation

- Narrowing solution choice

- Solution evaluation

- Road map

- Summary

Refresher and Restate the Challenge

Prior to beginning the solution space exercises that are held during the Design Thinking workshop, there is normally a break. The break could be overnight, during lunch, or for snacks or other reasons depending on the length of the problem space part of the workshop. Participants could begin to exhibit sleepiness if they eat during the break or tiredness from working on the earlier problem definition.

A refresher activity can help participants reengage before diving back into the workshop. These exercises typically involve standing up and some sort of physical movement to increase oxygen intake, thus clearing the brain and combatting sleepiness or tiredness. Examples of exercises that we use include

- Stand and stretch

- Stand and create new dance moves

- Stand, walk around the room twice, and sit down

- Play rock paper scissors with neighbors where winners continue to play until there is a room winner

Participants will now be ready to take another look at problem challenge statements that were selected. Facilitators might invite the key stakeholder or another participant to restate them for the room. They might also lead a conversation to confirm everyone agrees these are the most important topics to focus on.

Note   All the teams might be working on a single problem, or one or more teams might choose to work on different problems depending on goals for the workshop.

Facilitators must use this prelude to build consensus and ensure that the participants are alert and ready to move on. They should remind participants that they are about to start the fun part of the workshop where they get to create solutions.

Getting Inspiration

We begin by exploring inspiration methods that help participants begin to consider ways of solving problems from likely and unlikely sources prior to ideation. The methods that we will describe in this section are as follows:

- Beginner's mind

- Review data and research

- Outside perspective

- Lightning demos

- Inspiration landscape

The goal is to use these methods to stoke idea generation and encourage participants think outside of their immediate boundaries.

Method: Beginner's Mind

The beginner's mind is a concept from Zen Buddhism. It is described as having an attitude of openness, eagerness, and lack of preconceptions when studying a subject, even when studying the subject at an advanced level. The subject is approached as a beginner would.

Embracing a beginner's mindset enables one to stay open to any topic or experience no matter how advanced their knowledge becomes. It is the opposite of thinking that one knows everything about a topic and is centered on the idea that having some knowledge is not enough.

A good place for participants to start is to embrace more openness in understanding the problem space. They should be encouraged by the facilitator to look at what was previously uncovered with fresh eyes. This helps remove bias and clouded prejudgments or preconceptions and fantasies about the nature of the problem and what the solution could be. The format is usually an open discussion lasting from 10 to 30 minutes.

An open mindset should lead participants to put more focus on listening, becoming curious, asking more questions, and embracing not knowing. They will likely be more satisfied as they take part in the exercises in the workshop and formulate new ideas with other participants. This approach should help everyone gain a deeper understanding of the problem that needs to be solved.

This activity can seem foreign to some and takes practice. But it can be very worthwhile leading to more elegant, inclusive, and impactful ideas.

Method: Review Data and Research

An open mindset can drive participants to want to return to the exploration work performed at the beginning of the workshop and review the challenges present and the problem that really needs to be solved. There could be additional data and research available that could help. The data could be quantitative or qualitative and provide new inspiration.

Note   Quantitative data provides actual quantities and status, reflecting what is really happening. A few examples include data items, such as orders, delivery dates and pricing, process flow status, and data held in activity logs. Qualitative data describes why events are occurring by depicting them in their natural settings and can be used to interpret the meanings that people bring. For example, qualitative data might include sentiment, purpose, and reasons for behavior and can be captured in interviews, reviews, and questionnaires.

Both types of data are useful in fully understanding what is happening. For instance, in the supply chain optimization example that was introduced earlier in this book, we might know through quantitative data that plant managers and plant operations personnel have stopped ordering parts from a certain supplier, choosing instead to use alternative suppliers. This does not tell us why they stopped using that supplier. Qualitative "feeling" or "behavior" data can help pinpoint where the dissatisfaction lies and will hint at ways to remediate it. Here, we might uncover that there is a poor relationship between the supplier's sales representative and the plant manager.

A discussion at this point about the data and research is usually led by the facilitator and/or sponsor and varies in length from 10 to 30 minutes. If additional exploration is determined to be needed, the beginning of solution space exploration might be delayed appropriately, but the insight gained could be well worth it.

Method: Outside Perspective

We can gain the perspective of those outside of the organization by inviting them to review the information already gathered in the workshop and to offer their opinions. An outside perspective can help to assure objectivity and provide new perceptions and ideas that are not subject to internal orthodoxies and norms. It can help eliminate the mindset of "that's how it has always been done," remove bias, and help the organization get outside of its comfort zone.

We might solicit insights from partners, consultants, customers, and those who work in related industries. This feedback can help us learn from the mistakes of others and discover how others have solved problems like the challenges that are being faced.

When the problem to be solved is specific to customers or partners, it is particularly useful to have them engaged. They will understand the context of the problem and offer additional considerations that we might not have thought of. They can also help to define a better solution when brought into this process.

The need for such outside review is a good thing to discuss in prior to the Design Thinking workshop as it gives the facilitator time to set up appropriate conference call meetings and invite the right participants. Reviews at this stage are usually about 30 minutes in length.

Method: Lightning Demos

Lightning demos are an informal way to get a good understanding of what is already available as a solution. The exercise begins with having participants within each team make a list of various products and services that can inspire a solution (taking no more than 20 minutes). Participants are encouraged to think outside of their field or industry when making their lists to help ensure that they are not simply copying competitors.

Once the lists are complete, each participant gives a 3-minute talk within their team about one of the solutions on their list. The participant describes why the solution that they selected is compelling and how it applies to the current problem space.

As presentations are given, a scribe takes notes. Visuals might also be created that represent the ideas being described. Votes can be taken regarding continuing to explore these solutions during the second half of the workshop.

Method: Inspiration Landscape

You might instead be asked to evaluate approaches previously used within your organization, by competitors, and outsiders not in your industry related to the problem that you are trying to solve. We will refer to these individuals here as the players. This information can be gathered into an inspiration landscape worksheet or similar document. (The XPLANE website has their version of the worksheet publicly available for downloading at `https://x.xplane.com/inspiration_landscape_worksheet`.)

When performed as a team exercise, each team will draw a version of the worksheet on a sticky sheet that will have rows representing the status of the three types of players being evaluated. A column to the right of each player type lists the good, positive, or interesting things that the player is known for relative to the problem. A column farthest to the right lists the bad things that we likely want to avoid as it is populated with problems, issues, and the lessons learned. When a diverse and knowledgeable team works on filling it out, the exercise usually takes about 30 minutes.

We have come up with our own variation regarding how the sheet is labeled and created a version shown in Figure 4-1. This sheet reflects the state of supplier relationships and supply chain management within different players in our example. We can readily see that competition is likely using some best practices when it comes to data given that they are fast followers of others, even though they are not great at making predictions. We can also see that the outsiders do provide a potential threat to ourselves (and possibly to suppliers) as they have lots data and use it wisely, though they are currently willing to share it.

Players	What is good	Not so good
Internal	• Strong personal supplier relationships • Bottoms up plant management creating innovation in certain plants	• Processes used with suppliers sometimes vary • Supply chain managed by gut feel • Suppliers often blindsided
Competition (Traditional)	• Fast followers of best practices • Respond more quickly to issues • Better margins	• Known for supplier churn • Not good at predicting supply chain issues though they have data
Outsiders (Potential threat)	• Seen as more innovative • Provide lots of data and analysis to suppliers • Can provide heads-up re: shortages	• Seen by suppliers as long term potential threat • Suppliers have difficulty maintaining their own margins

Figure 4-1. Inspiration landscape for the supply chain optimization example

Understanding Innovation Ambition

Before gathering ideas regarding how we might solve the identified problem, we might want to gage the innovation ambition tolerance within the organization. This can help workshop teams understand where they should focus when defining potential solutions. They should understand if their ideas for solutions are expected to be disruptive and highly strategic in their industry, solve an immediate crisis that is highly tactical, or span the broad spectrum.

A means of classifying where solution ideas might fit is described as an innovation ambition matrix. It is described in an article published in May 2012 in the *Harvard Business Review* (see the Appendix for a link to the source). The matrix describes the three kinds of initiatives that organizations typically undertake as being core, adjacent, or transformational.

Figure 4-2 represents the innovation ambition matrix.

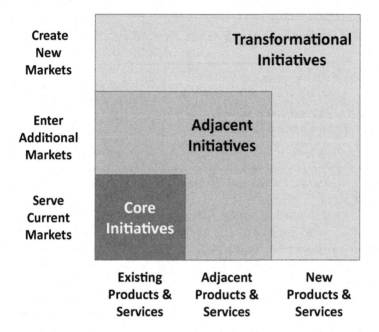

Figure 4-2. *Innovation ambition matrix*

Core initiatives provide small incremental innovation that improves an existing product or service offering. For example, converting a manual process that is currently accomplished on paper to digital would be considered core. Other examples include packaging changes or simple design modifications to an existing product. These are valuable initiatives but are not considered revolutionary to a business segment or to an industry.

More adventurous ideas are labeled as adjacent initiatives. In these initiatives, the organization enters adjacent markets and serves new customers by modifying existing products and offerings to provide needed capabilities. This approach enables the organization to extend their current resources and skills to serve the expanded audience in a whole different way.

At the far end of the spectrum are transformational initiatives, often considered to be true game changers. The organization creates entirely new products to service new markets that they create. For these initiatives to be successful, there must be a willingness to invest in new assets, skills, and development of the markets. When successfully accomplished, these can provide an organization with a first to market advantage as well as enabling a whole new business.

The facilitator can draw the innovation ambition matrix figure or use a printed copy to reference as they lead a discussion about the types of initiatives that could be considered viable in the organization. This 20- to 30-minute discussion will help the teams focus on developing solution ideas that are more likely to be adopted. If the organization is looking for ideas beyond those found in core initiatives, it can also help spur participants to think outside of their traditional boundaries.

Solution Ideation

We are now ready to begin solution ideation. Our goal is to expand the thinking and ideas of everyone on the team but also create something that is greater than the sum of the parts. Entering this divergent phase of the solution space, we want to gather as many ideas as possible from everyone.

The method that we use to generate solution ideas is called the creative matrix.

Method: Creative Matrix

The creative matrix is a tool that will help spark ideas that are formed at intersections with discrete categories. The matrix is formulated based on who the solution must serve and the criteria being used to define it.

Each team writes their problem statement (how might we...) at the top of a sticky easel sheet to begin the exercise and then draws a grid. Each cell will represent the intersection of people for whom the solution could be relevant and business enablers. The grid columns are defined as the groups of people for whom the intended solution is relevant (e.g., personas, market segments, or unique stakeholders).

Rows are then defined by categories of criteria believed relevant for enabling potential solutions. Some examples of categories that might be considered as relevant include

- Technology and digital media (analytical solutions, IoT devices, phones, tablets, watches, and lifestyle trackers)

- Environments and interfaces (physical conditions, human requirements, engagement of senses, visualizations, and gamification)

- Internal policies, procedures, and processes (also including incentives and training)

- Public policies and laws (also including unwritten customs, upcoming legislation, and policy platforms)

- Partnerships required (distribution and sales channels, suppliers, and consultants)

- A wildcard category that could be used for ideas not fitting into the defined categories

Once a team's grid is laid out, each participant is given a pen and a sticky note pad. They are asked to think of solutions to the identified problem that would be appropriate at intersections of the categories and solution audience. They write one idea per sticky note and stick it into the appropriate cell. Ideas that do not fit in any cell are put into a parking lot. This exercise should be limited to 30 minutes in length.

When every cell has been filled in or the time limit has been reached, teams huddle around their creative matrix and review the ideas. If multiple teams are working on the same problem, they might also review matrixes created by other teams. Each participant is then asked to vote on their favorite solution idea (or top two or top three) by placing a sticker or dot on the sticky note(s). The sticky notes with the most votes become the most promising solutions to further evaluate.

Note   Just like we did in the abstraction ladder method that we described in Chapter 3, we use a combination of brainstorming and voting in the creative matrix method to generate ideas. The goal of brainstorming is to produce a large quantity of ideas in a facilitated, judgment-free environment. Since the voting on the solution ideas is subjective, we will apply additional methods to assess the proposed solutions when we seek to narrow our choices.

Figure 4-3 illustrates a creative matrix prepared using our supply chain optimization example. The statement "How might we improve plant operations for plant management by understanding supply chain shortages" appears in the upper left. Relevant parties with a stake in this solution include plant management, sales, supply chain logistics, and executive management. Categories denoted here are technology, visualizations, processes, and wildcards. (Category labels are sometimes adjusted to align with solutions that the participants think of during this exercise.)

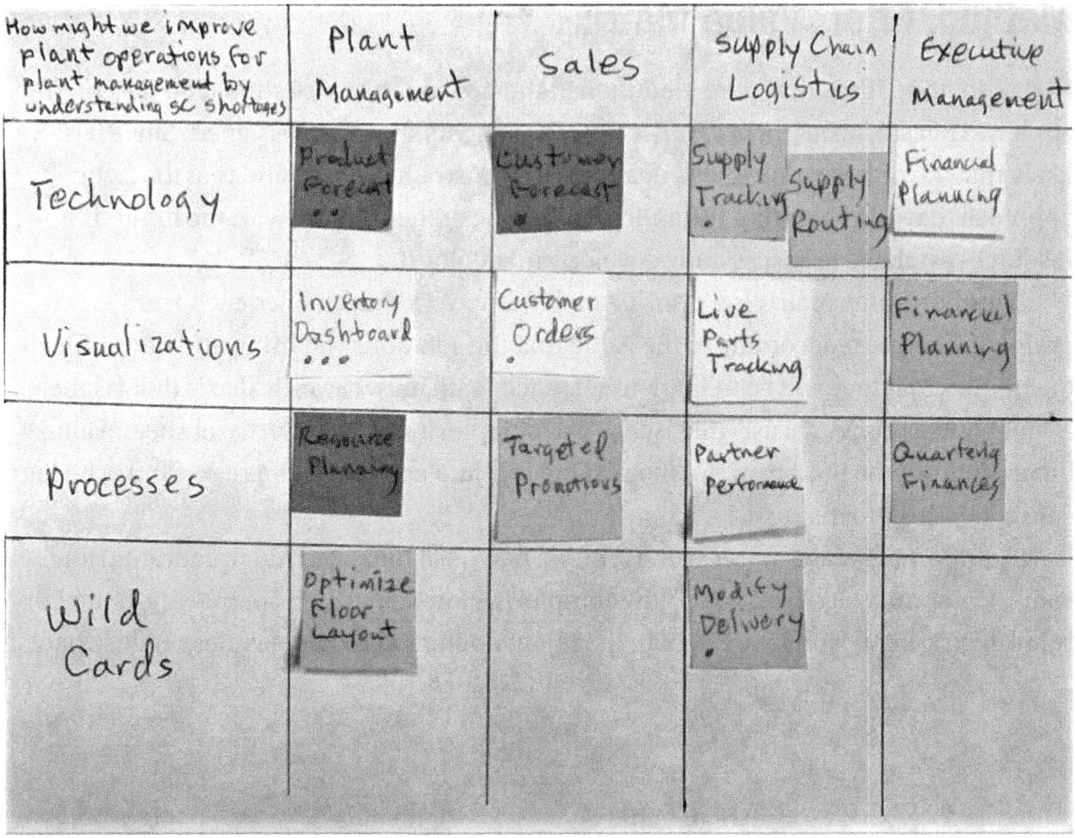

How might we improve plant operations for plant management by understanding sc shortages	Plant Management	Sales	Supply Chain Logistics	Executive Management
Technology	Product Forecast	Customer Forecast	Supply Tracking / Supply Routing	Financial Planning
Visualizations	Inventory Dashboard	Customer Orders	Live Parts Tracking	Financial Planning
Processes	Resource Planning	Targeted Promotions	Partner Performance	Quarterly Finances
Wild Cards	Optimize Floor Layout		Modify Delivery	

Figure 4-3. *Creative matrix representing supply chain optimization example*

We can see that the inventory dashboard solution received the most votes, but there was also interest in forecasting applied to product demand (especially the associated parts) and customer demand, tracking supplies (in transit), and modifying the type of delivery for certain parts.

Narrowing Solution Choice

Next, we must converge upon fewer solutions for each problem under consideration. (In some workshops, multiple solutions to a single problem are pursued with competing teams developing those approaches.) We prioritize the solutions under consideration and begin planning how we might move forward. To provide clarity regarding what the solution(s) consist of, we also need to provide visualizations. Methods in this section describe the effort value matrix and visualizations, including storyboards and concept posters.

Method: Effort Value Matrix

Not all solution ideas that were identified in the previous exercise should be weighted equally. That said, you might wonder how the weights should be assigned. Since it is likely that the organization is also dealing with constraints, many find that the right approach to use is balancing the anticipated value of the solution with the limited resources available to successfully develop and deploy it.

The effort value matrix is a prioritization framework that enables each team to evaluate their ideas according to the value that the solutions will bring and how difficult or complex that they will be to implement. Each team draws a vertical axis that is labeled "value" and a horizontal axis that is labeled "complexity" on a sticky easel sheet. Value increases from the bottom of the sheet to the top, and complexity increases from the left side of the sheet to the right.

Figure 4-4 illustrates these axes. Here, we have also indicated four quadrants (low value/low complexity, high value/low complexity, low value/high complexity, and high value/high complexity) that illustrate the relative values and complexities on this chart.

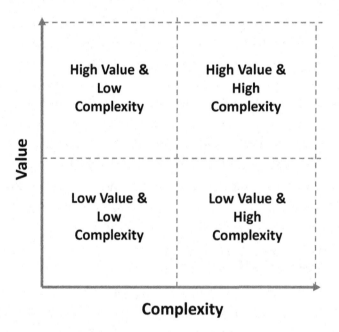

Figure 4-4. *Effort value matrix*

Next, the teams take their solutions sticky notes and place them in the appropriate quadrants and relative to each other on the chart. A best practice is to first place them along the value axis to understand that relative positioning and then move them into appropriate complexity positioning, maintaining their value stack rank order.

The matrix should help us see some low business value/high complexity solutions that we want to avoid implementing. The "low hanging fruit" solutions are those in the low complexity/high business value quadrant. That said, we might still place a high priority on certain high business value/high complexity initiatives, particularly if they are transformative, and that is a goal that we have identified. Thus, as we consider a solution road map, we will focus on solutions in these two quadrants.

Figure 4-5 shows the results of this exercise using our supply chain optimization example. We have placed the solutions that received votes during our work on the creative matrix method onto an effort value matrix.

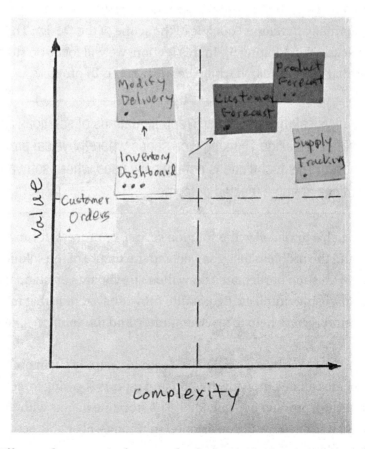

Figure 4-5. *Effort value matrix for supply chain optimization example*

The leading vote getter, the inventory dashboard, appears in the high value/low complexity quadrant. The arrows pointed at modify delivery and toward the forecasting solutions are used to indicate that we believe that the inventory dashboard and customer orders must be created prior to building these other solutions.

Our experience is that while this exercise can take as little as 5 minutes, longer discussions of 15 to 20 minutes can be quite worthwhile when relative values and complexities of solutions are debated and ascertained.

Method: Visualizations

A solution defined by a sticky note does an inadequate job of conveying the intent of the visionary behind the solution, how the solution will be utilized, and the value that it can provide. While a more detailed description can be written, a picture is often worth a thousand words.

There are several ways to visualize the solution. In software and AI projects, prototypes are normally developed outside of the scope of the Design Thinking workshop (as discussed in Chapter 5). In this section, we will focus on storyboards and concept posters that can be created while the workshop is in progress.

Note   Simple physical models that are representations of solutions are sometimes created in Design Thinking workshops where physical products are being proposed. This technique is not typically used where software and AI developed solutions are an expected outcome.

A storyboard helps to visualize the solution service or process. It can help viewers quickly understand the problem being solved and the nature of the solution within a specific context. Workshop participants draw their storyboards on standard sheets of paper or notecards, using simplistic figures and providing a dialog that mimics a comic strip to tell their story. These help the viewer understand the solution's value, usability, and application.

Figure 4-6 shows a storyboard created to illustrate a supply chain optimization solution that includes an inventory dashboard and reports showing forecasts of customer demand and product parts needed. The storyline begins with the problem and challenges and then shows how the envisioned solutions will enable actions to be taken to mitigate the problem.

Figure 4-6. *Storyboard for supply chain optimization example solution*

Creating the storyboard usually takes about 15 to 20 minutes. When complete, a best practice is to have each participant read and show their storyboard. A vote is sometimes taken to choose the best one.

Concept posters are used to promote and explain a solution. The poster denotes what the solution is called and provides a solution illustration, a description of key stakeholders, a list of features and benefits, and a simplistic road map or timeline. It can be used to begin to gain agreement on the business need for the solution.

Figure 4-7 illustrates a concept poster for our supply chain optimization solution.

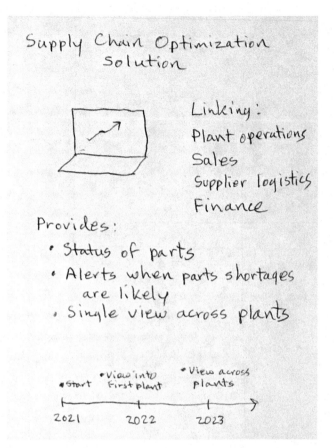

Figure 4-7. *Concept poster for supply chain optimization example solution*

Concept posters usually take a bit longer to develop than storyboards (about 45 minutes is typical). As with storyboards, each participant might be asked to present their poster and a vote can be taken to choose the best one.

Solution Evaluation

As we near the end of the workshop, we could want to test some of our solution assumptions. We can do this through the following methods:

- Outside feedback and iteration

- Testable hypothesis

- Value map framework

Our goal in doing this is to validate that we are on the right track before too much time and effort is put into subsequent steps beyond the Design Thinking workshop.

Method: Outside Feedback and Iteration

The solution that you are bringing forward can provide a great starting point to a development project. However, gathering outside critiques of the solution's goals and functionality could lead to identifying a better workflow, improve usability, and grow the potential value.

Critical feedback is most effective when it is audible, actionable, and credible. It drives constructive discussion, removes blind spots, highlights opportunities for improvement, and builds alignment. One should not ask someone if they "like" the proposed solution as that will often only receive a polite "yes" and not make the solution better. Feedback requests require more structure to ensure that useful insight is obtained.

Outside feedback can be solicited from within the workshop or after the workshop ends. If solicited from within the workshop, this can involve providing remote conferencing into the workshop site. A review at this stage will likely require at least 30 minutes.

Keep in mind that whether you share solution progress from within the workshop or after, you need to have the right audience providing feedback. Try getting feedback from future users of the intended solution, especially if they are not present in the workshop, as they have a lot at stake. Also, solicit feedback from additional business stakeholders who might not be targeted to use the solution but who understand its potential importance to the business. Lastly, consider reviewing the solution with people who do not understand why it is needed. They might need a more in-depth explanation of the problem and the solution but that could provide insights that the others cannot provide.

The following steps can be used to ensure that constructive feedback is received:

- Gain a commitment that honest feedback will be provided.

- Explain the business problem space and the impact of not solving this problem.

- Describe the solution using visualizations to help explain options.

- Encourage the reviewer to ask clarifying questions during the presentation and avoid responding in a defensive manner.

- After the presentation, ask the reviewer if there are any other questions and, once again, avoid responding in a defensive manner.

- Ask for specific feedback about what they liked and why, simply taking notes while they speak.

- Ask for feedback about what they did not like or what they found confusing or challenging, again simply taking notes.

- Ask if they have any ideas for improvements and ask clarifying questions as needed.

- Thank them and tell them that the gift of honest feedback will make the solution better.

The more comprehensive feedback that is received, the better the solution can become. A group that provides outside feedback can become a group of advocates when their suggestions are incorporated into the solution and they might also become willing test candidates for the solution.

Method: Testable Hypothesis

Assumptions made during the workshop are not always correct. If certain assumptions are driving the defined solution, it is a good idea to test their validity. If some of the assumptions are not valid, an adjustment in the solution might be required. Now is the time to explore these before solution development moves forward.

Our outside feedback group can be a useful audience when applying this method. Hypothesis statements are developed and provide a means of testing the assumptions. These statements take the form of "We believe that (a solution that serves someone) will deliver/is critical to (providing a benefit or value)" and "We will know that it is successful if (a measured success occurs)."

Using our supply chain optimization example, we could put one of our assumptions into the following statements:

- We believe that providing our suppliers with online access into our plant order status information is critical to eliminating parts shortages impacting our plant operators.

- We know that we are successful if expected delivery dates are met and our manufacturing line is no longer idle due to a parts shortage.

Thus, we stated the belief, why it is important, and who it impacts. Then, we describe what we expect to achieve and the evidence that we would collect to prove it true. If we were to find that there was no way to prove our hypothesis, we would likely be heading in the wrong direction since our outcome would be unclear.

Method: Value Map Framework

Earlier in the workshop when we created the effort value matrix, we gained consensus about the relative value of various potential solutions (as well as their complexity). However, we have not explored their absolute value, something that will become important when we later build a business case that will help justify funding a project.

A value map framework can be used to provide an analytical view of the value of the solution. Tangible benefits such as revenue growth, cost savings, and improved productivity can be predicted and subsequently measured as the solution is developed and tested. Other benefits such as market share maintenance and risk mitigation might be more difficult to prove but could also provide value.

To use this method, each team begins by coming up with a list of projected benefits. On a sticky sheet, they then write the name of the solution at the top and then create a grid with five columns. Columns are labeled as business outcomes, strategies, tactics, key performance indicators (KPIs), and technology capabilities. Rows are the expected business benefit outcomes. The business benefit outcomes are filled into the left-hand column. Team members then use sticky notes to populate the other columns appropriately. After about 30 minutes, each team presents its results to the other teams. If multiple teams are working on the same solution, a single value map framework is created that combines the results of all the efforts.

Figure 4-8 illustrates a value map framework for the supply chain optimization example where the business outcomes are revenue growth, cost savings, and improved productivity.

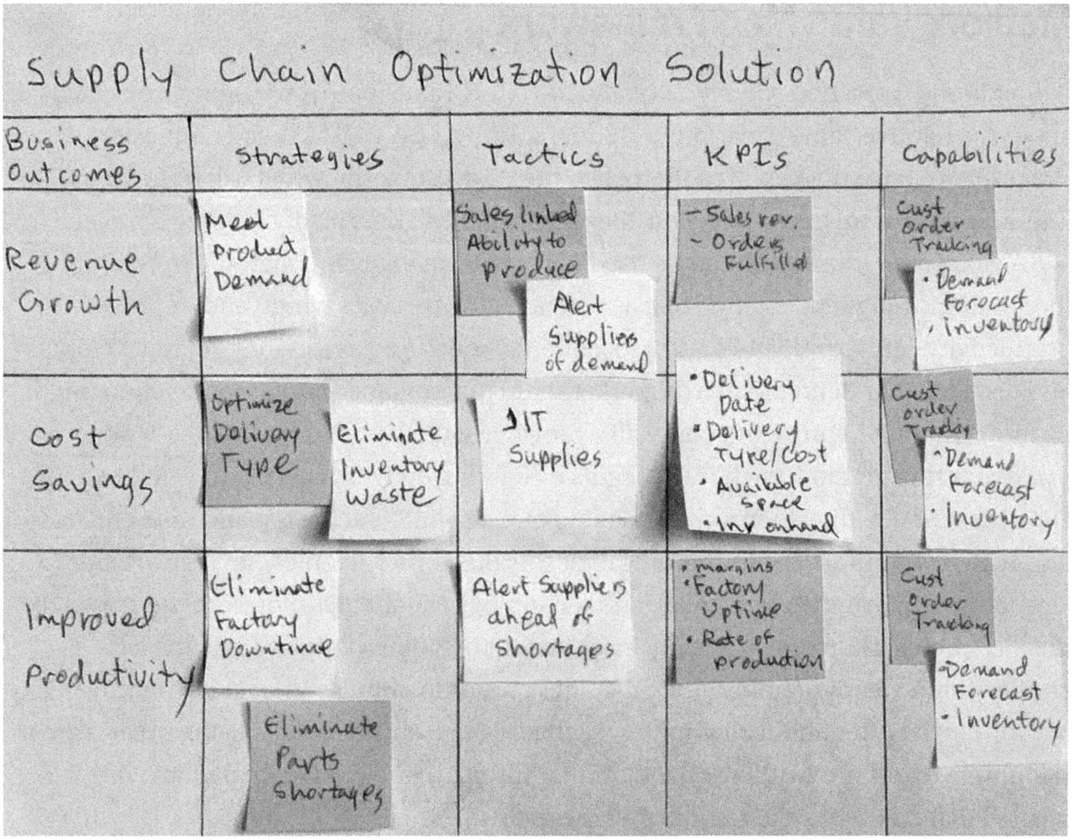

Supply Chain Optimization Solution

Business Outcomes	Strategies		Tactics	KPIs	Capabilities
Revenue Growth	Meet Product Demand		Sales linked Ability to produce / Alert Supplies of demand	– Sales rev. – Orders Fulfilld	Cust Order Tracking • Demand Forecast • Inventory
Cost Savings	Optimize Delivery Type	Eliminate Inventory waste	JIT Supplies	• Delivery Date • Delivery Type/Cost • Available Space • Inv onhand	Cust order Tracking • Demand Forecast • Inventory
Improved Productivity	Eliminate Factory Downtime	Eliminate Parts Shortages	Alert Supplies ahead of shortages	• margins • Factory Uptime • Rate of production	Cust order Tracking • Demand Forecast • Inventory

Figure 4-8. *Value map for supply chain optimization example*

Business value propositions should be able to be constructed into small statements that can serve as the basis for a business case using this information. The tactics, KPIs, and capabilities should help drive the prototype creation activity after the workshop concludes.

Note   Now that we have identified some of the KPIs required, we could build another visualization that would serve as a mockup of a potential dashboard. This could be used to help guide prototype creation after the workshop ends.

Road Map and Close

The final step in a Design Thinking workshop is creation of a list of next steps that will provide a road map of solution development moving forward. Typically, one to three solutions are chosen to pursue further at this point. A key goal of this exercise is to gain commitment from participants to continue developing the solution(s). This step is led by the facilitator with all participants engaged in providing input.

We suggest that the following format should be adopted when capturing next steps planned for the top solution ideas. List each solution idea, and then provide a description of each. Be sure to reference any visuals created (such as the storyboard or concept poster) that help to explain the solution. Then indicate immediate tasks that need to be accomplished. Also indicate other tasks to follow next, and then tasks that need to be accomplished later. Assign an owner of the tasks who will be held accountable and lead the effort for each. Deadlines might also be noted for tasks when the scope for each is understood.

Note   A facilitator might start gathering a list of next steps, including tasks and owners, prior to the end of the workshop. If that has occurred along the way, use this time at the end of the workshop to review the list and modify it as needed to define the road map.

In Figure 4-9, we illustrate a partial example of a road map task list that would define steps after the supply chain optimization solution workshop. We see that there are immediate plans to refine the list of KPIs, assess the data that is available to the organization, and review the Design Thinking workshop content with executive management. The "do next" tasks then build upon the "do now" list and include creating a prototype.

Solution : Supply Chain Optimization

Description: Provides a means to mitigate parts shortages by tracking Inventory, orders, and predicting demand. storyboard & concept poster availabl

Do Now	Do Next	Do Later	Owner
• Refine KPIs needed	• Feedback to Data Science		Plant Manager
• Assess available data	• Rationalize data with KPIs		Data Scientist
	• Build prototype	• Review with Lines of business	Data Scientist
• Review workshop output with executive management	• Incorporate Feedback into Summary of workshop		Sponsor

Figure 4-9. Road map of next steps for supply chain optimization example

The workshop can now conclude. The facilitator and sponsor(s) typically thank everyone for their time. The content from the workshop is then gathered into a small presentation to show what was accomplished. It is sent to participants along with another thank you note and the road map of what happens next.

Summary

In this chapter, we began with a prelude to the second portion of the Design Thinking workshop in which we discussed the importance of restating the challenge and methods for getting inspiration and understanding an organization's innovation ambition. The methods and discussions that we provided would be used if considered appropriate for your situation. The anticipated timing of each of them are as follows:

- Beginner's mind – 10 to 30 minutes

- Review data and research – 10 to 30 minutes

- Outside perspective – 30 minutes

- Lightning demos – 20 minutes to gather content, 3 minutes each present

- Inspiration landscape – 30 minutes

- Innovation ambition – 20- to 30-minute discussion

We then explored the solution space, beginning with solution ideation, then narrowed to a single or a few solutions, performed solution(s) evaluation, and then described building a road map of next steps beyond the workshop. The methods that can be used in this portion of the workshop include

- Creative matrix – 30 minutes

- Effort value matrix – 15 to 20 minutes

- Visualizations – 45 minutes

- Outside feedback and iteration – 30-minute (minimum) discussion

- Testable hypothesis – 20-minute discussion

- Value map framework – 30 minutes

- Road map – 30-minute discussion

Like the timing of the problem space exploration, the length of time for the solution space portion is variable depending on the number of teams and participants. You should plan on at least half a day for this portion of the workshop. Inclusion of multiple methods for reflection prior to starting solution space exploration and inviting outside parties for reviews via conference call meetings can greatly lengthen it.

You should now understand what is gained through a Design Thinking workshop and how the workshop is executed. In Chapter 5, we cover a logical next step in the development of many software and AI solutions, the creation of a prototype.

CHAPTER 5

Prototype Creation

Now that we have used a Design Thinking approach to identify problems to be solved and then identified some appropriate potential solutions, we can begin creating technology-based prototypes to aid in the evaluation of these solutions. These technology prototypes can be viewed as early development attempts that might later evolve into full-fledged production-level solutions. At this stage, we need to control the scope of our development efforts and go just far enough to evaluate whether we are on the right track.

In this chapter, we begin by discussing possible prototyping approaches that we might use and then discuss the role of user interface prototypes and how they can guide our subsequent software and AI solutions development. We next evaluate whether pre-built applications might align to what is needed (with some customization) or whether the solution must be entirely custom-built. As we go through each of these steps, limiting the scope of these efforts will help us keep our stakeholders engaged.

We then explore where the solution might fit in our existing technology architecture and make use of available reference architectures as part of that effort. Finally, we take a deeper look at what takes place during prototype evaluation and describe some reasons why the evaluation might cause us to take another look at the potential solution.

The chapter contains the following major sections:

- Choosing a prototyping approach

- User interface prototypes

- Applications vs. custom build

- Reference architectures

- Prototype and solution evaluation

- Summary

© Robert Stackowiak and Tracey Kelly 2020
R. Stackowiak and T. Kelly, *Design Thinking in Software and AI Projects*

Choosing a Prototyping Approach

In Chapter 4, we introduced storyboards and mockups as part of the Design Thinking workshop. They provided a glimpse into what the desired potential solutions might provide and how they might be used. We did this to gain initial validation regarding the value of these solutions. After the Design Thinking workshop successfully concludes, we can begin prototype development using technology components. A prototype involving software will help drive more detailed specifications for full production design and development.

Software development life cycle (SDLC) models for prototypes are generally classified as either being rapid prototypes that are throwaway or as evolutionary prototypes that will change over time and become more aligned to user requirements as they become better known. Our earlier storyboards and mockups might be considered as very early stage throwaway prototypes serving as a prelude to taking an evolutionary approach incorporating software.

As prototypes are developed in software, our stakeholders and frontline workers will review them and suggest changes (or possibly suggest discarding the prototype entirely and starting anew if it doesn't align at all to the solution that is needed). After several iterations using this approach, the prototype might be deemed as acceptable in delivering the scope of the solution that was envisioned. We can then move beyond this stage.

Note   Some organizations choose to begin by developing a broad line-of-business solution prototype designed to impact all relevant business areas. They later focus on developing additional prototypes that provide line-of-business specific solutions. Others start by building prototype solutions within individual lines of business, sometimes working on these in parallel. They then create a cross line-of-business solution prototype by gathering the relevant data and output from the individual lines of business. The best approach to use depends on who the most important stakeholders are and where one can most quickly deliver prototypes that will demonstrate the potential value of the solution.

In all efforts, there is a need to collect relevant data required to demonstrate the prototype. In AI and machine learning projects, having real validated data directly impacts the success of prototype development. As a result, an early evaluation of data cleanliness and completeness is usually necessary in those types of projects.

In typical AI and machine learning projects, algorithms for developing early models are selected, the models are trained and tested, and the results are shared with stakeholders and frontline workers. Upon evaluation, a decision is made to further optimize the process (as needed) and move on or to repeat the process to improve the envisioned solution accuracy.

Today, prototype development increasingly takes place using cloud-based resources. Reasons often given for this transition from on-premise development to the cloud include

- Faster access to needed software and AI resources

- An ability to spin up or spin down additional storage and processing resources with a pay as you go processing model

- An ability to support production-level workloads when moving beyond the prototype stage

- Well-understood security capabilities that become especially important later when development efforts transition into production

User Interface Prototypes

Prototype development will often begin with a focus on the user interface since stakeholders can more easily relate to the usefulness of the solution when data is presented to them in this form. The data will sometimes come from spreadsheets already being used by frontline workers or other readily available data sources. Where such data is not readily available, datasets simulating real data are sometimes substituted.

Reports and dashboards are prepared that mimic the production-level solutions that will be built later. Automated actions (such as the sending of alerts, emails, and other triggers) might also be developed or simulated and demonstrated to stakeholders.

In our supply chain example, the following metrics need to be tracked by management so that they can make decisions that will optimize plant production and prevent supply shortages or excess inventory:

- Key suppliers for products and the product components that they supply

- Ratings of suppliers (based on previous orders delivered on time)

- Components currently on hand within the plant(s)

- Components on order including order status and expected delivery dates

- Components in transit from suppliers to the plant(s)

- Incoming product orders for the plant(s) with promised delivery dates

- Anticipated component shortfalls, surplus, and timeline

We can begin developing a user interface prototype by using small sample datasets. An Excel-based dataset is illustrated in Figure 5-1. It identifies the product being manufactured, the supplier of a specific part, the part, the number of units purchased, the price per part, the purchase amount of the order, the date the order occurred, the scheduled delivery date, and the delivery type.

	A	B	C	D	E	F	G	H	I
1	Product	Supplier	Part	Units Purchased	Price per Part	Purchase Amount	Date Ordered	Scheduled Delivery	Delivery Type
2	Widget assembly	ABC	ABA220	500	$ 20.00	$ 20,000.00	1/2/2020	3/15/2020	Express Air
3	Widget assembly	Aardvark	ABA220	550	$ 20.00	$ 22,000.00	1/2/2020	4/15/2020	Delivery Truck
4	Widget assembly	XYZ	Frame100	600	$ 350.00	$ 420,000.00	1/5/2020	3/5/2020	Delivery Truck
5	Widget assembly	Pieceparts	ZZ40404	800	$ 7.00	$ 11,200.00	1/5/2020	3/16/2020	Regular Air
6	Widget assembly	Hwparts	ZZ40404	600	$ 125.00	$ 150,000.00	1/5/2020	3/18/2020	Regular Air
7	Widget assembly	ABC	XNS221	550	$ 12.00	$ 13,200.00	1/31/2020	3/15/2020	Regular Air
8	Widget assembly	Blondie	Frame100	400	$ 325.00	$ 260,000.00	2/10/2020	4/19/2020	Delivery Truck
9	Widget assembly	Elmo	XNS221	450	$ 13.00	$ 11,700.00	2/15/2020	4/30/2020	Regular Air
10	Widget assembly	ABC	ABA230	450	$ 15.00	$ 13,500.00	6/1/2020	8/1/2020	Regular Air
11	Widget assembly	Aardvark	ABA230	275	$ 15.00	$ 8,250.00	6/1/2020	8/1/2020	Regular Air
12	Widget assembly	Elmo	ABA230	200	$ 15.00	$ 6,000.00	6/1/2020	8/15/2020	Delivery Truck
13	Widget assembly	ABC	XNS231	300	$ 12.00	$ 7,200.00	6/1/2020	8/1/2020	Regular Air
14	Widget assembly	Elmo	XNS231	550	$ 10.00	$ 11,000.00	6/1/2020	8/5/2020	Regular Air
15	Widget assembly	Pieceparts	ZZ40404	400	$ 9.00	$ 7,200.00	6/2/2020	8/8/2020	Regular Air
16	Widget assembly	Hwparts	ZZ40404	200	$ 300.00	$ 120,000.00	6/3/2020	8/15/2020	Regular Air
17	Widget assembly	XYZ	Frame100-1	615	$ 295.00	$ 362,850.00	6/6/2020	8/15/2020	Delivery Truck
18	Widget assembly	Blondie	Frame100-1	303	$ 297.00	$ 179,982.00	6/7/2020	8/20/2020	Delivery Truck

Figure 5-1. *Sample supplier, parts, and orders data*

When tabular reports and visualizations are created to serve as user interfaces using sample datasets, they are reviewed with key stakeholders and frontline workers prior to further prototype development. Each group will likely want to focus on certain information that directly impacts their ability to make decisions, especially if it also impacts their ability to meet personal and broader business goals, provides opportunities for career advancement, and drives their compensation.

In our example, the plant managers and the CFO (who monitors contracts with suppliers) indicated that they want to see the number of parts and the delivery dates for each of the orders initiated with suppliers. Using a business intelligence tool and the sample dataset, we can create a tabular report by selecting the appropriate data fields. For illustrative purposes, we used the Microsoft Power BI Desktop to produce the output that is shown in Figure 5-2.

Supplier	Part	Units Purchased	Month	Day
Aardvark	ABA220	550	April	15
Aardvark	ABA230	275	August	1
ABC	ABA220	500	March	15
ABC	ABA230	450	August	1
ABC	XNS221	550	March	15
ABC	XNS231	300	August	1
Blondie	Frame100	400	April	19
Blondie	Frame100-1	303	August	20
Elmo	ABA230	200	August	15
Elmo	XNS221	450	April	30
Elmo	XNS231	550	August	5
Hwparts	ZZ40404	600	March	18
Hwparts	ZZ40404	200	August	15
Pieceparts	ZZ40404	800	March	16
Pieceparts	ZZ40404	400	August	8
XYZ	Frame100	600	March	5
XYZ	Frame100-1	615	August	15

Figure 5-2. *Tabular report showing suppliers, parts, units, and delivery dates*

The plant managers and CFO also expressed an interest in seeing the total number of units expected from each supplier to better understand their share of providing critical parts. The pie chart visualization provided by Power BI gives us a nice way to quickly understand the distribution.

As shown in Figure 5-3, we can observe that there is a somewhat even volume distribution of units provided by the suppliers. As viewed here, supplier ABC provides the most parts (23 percent) and Blondie the fewest (9 percent) with others falling in between.

Of greater interest to plant managers and the CFO is understanding the amount of spending with each supplier. This is represented in Figure 5-4.

Units Purchased by Supplier

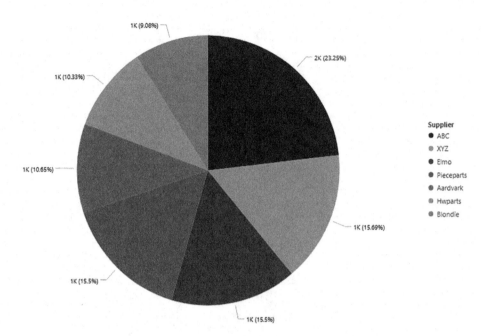

Figure 5-3. *Share of number of parts provided by each supplier*

In Figure 5-4, we clearly see that the supplier where the most money is spent is vendor XYZ (48 percent of the supplier spend). Vendor Blondie is second (27 percent). This should probably be expected as they make frames, the most expensive parts in the sample dataset. A plant manager and the CFO would likely look at Figures 5-3 and 5-4 and request the ability to view by part number the vendor share of units and money spent. This would make it easier to do head-to-head comparisons of suppliers of the same parts.

Purchase Amount by Supplier

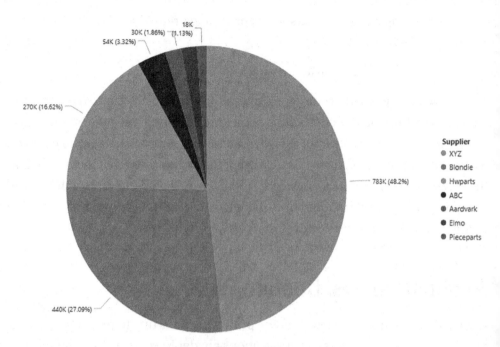

Figure 5-4. *Share of spending with each supplier*

After gathering feedback and modifying the reports and visualizations as needed, they can be published for wider distribution and further reviewed and utilized. They can also be inserted into dashboards that include many different reports and visualizations representing output from multiple datasets. Thus, a dashboard can provide a consolidated view of the entire situation enabling faster decision-making when solving the identified business problem.

As prototypes of reports, visualizations, and dashboards are widely reviewed, a list of further requirements is gathered. Typical items on the list often include the following requests for changes:

- Drilling to greater detail

- Viewing or visualizing the data in additional ways

- Adding more data (e.g., providing a longer history or additional data sources)

- Cleansing the data present

- Adding functionality (such as providing predictive capabilities or automated alerts)

- Deployment to a wider group of users

Given that we are at a prototype stage, adding artificially created data and/or simulating additional functionality is sometimes deemed adequate at this time.

Though user interfaces can excite your audiences and lead them to believe that a production solution is near, it is important to remind them that they are looking at just a prototype. If you are a developer, you likely realize that much of the work is just beginning. But you now should have gained solid direction on what is important to each audience that you are developing for.

Applications vs. Custom Build

At this point, we might believe that the prototype is starting to resemble an off-the-shelf application. When off-the-shelf applications are deployed in a cloud environment, they are referred to as Software-as-a-Service (SaaS) offerings.

SaaS offerings remove significant requirements regarding IT's involvement in deployment. SaaS providers are responsible for configuring and managing the applications, data, and underlying data management platforms, middleware, operating systems, virtualization, servers and storage, and networking. This can greatly speed time to implementation of these solutions and simplify support.

There are trade-offs that should be evaluated since the available applications may or may not closely align to the envisioned solution and could have limited flexibility in addressing the organization's unique needs. It is a good idea to perform a gap analysis comparing what is required and what the SaaS application provides. As the analysis is performed, consider currently mandated requirements and possible future or deferred requirements.

Using our supply chain optimization example, we could choose to evaluate an off-the-shelf application designed to perform this task. Based on requirements that we uncovered during the Design Thinking workshop and early prototype development, we might evaluate the application's ability to provide some or all the following functionality:

- Measure shortages and excess inventory within plants.

- Predict shortages and excess inventory within plants.

- Measure and manage shortages and excess inventory across multiple plants.

- Predict shortages and excess inventory across multiple plants.

- Alert plant managers as to emerging shortages or excess inventory.

- Manage relationships with multiple suppliers.

- Measure and rate suppliers based on previous on-time delivery performance.

- Alert suppliers as to emerging shortages or excess inventory.

- Set production goals within/across plants and measure outcomes.

- Evaluate multiple production objectives and plans simultaneously.

- Report using data from existing OLTP applications such as those used for demand management, order fulfillment, manufacturing management, supplier relationship management, and/or returns management.

- Report using real-time manufacturing data from the plant floor.

- Report using real-time supplies location data.

- Provide multi-language support for plants/suppliers around the world.

- Provide multi-currency support for plants/suppliers around the world.

Organizations typically involve key stakeholders in performing the gap analysis since they will understand the business implications of how the application operates and impact of functionality that is missing. Sometimes, as stakeholders better understand the capabilities that an application provides, new areas of interest are uncovered beyond what was defined as the problem and the desired solution in the Design Thinking workshop.

Note   There is a danger of scope creep when evaluating the functionality provided by applications. Controlling the scope of the prototype development effort should remain top of mind. Staying true to the defined problem and solution definition identified in the Design Thinking workshop can help keep the project on track.

Developing and deploying custom solutions removes functionality limitations that could be present in applications, but also requires a more significant effort. When creating custom solutions, many choose to deploy using Platform-as-a-Service (PaaS) offerings from cloud vendors. The cloud vendor is then responsible for configuring and managing the underlying data management platforms, middleware, operating systems, virtualization, servers and storage, and networking. The organization that is building the custom solution assumes ownership of configuring and managing their applications and data.

Yet more flexibility is provided by Infrastructure-as-a-Service (IaaS) cloud-based offerings. Organizations can mix and match components from a wider variety of vendors and deploy them upon a choice of cloud platforms. However, greater configuration, management, and integration ownership is placed upon the IT organization. Though deploying IaaS components was very common in the earlier years of cloud adoption, more recently PaaS has gained significant mindshare by simplifying the role of IT in these efforts.

What might an architecture look like supporting a software and AI project deployed to the cloud? We explore a couple of common reference architectures in the next section.

Reference Architectures

A reference architecture can provide a technology template for a potential software and AI solution. Adopting a reference architecture can also help an organization adopt a common vocabulary used in describing key components and lead them toward proven best practices routinely used when deploying similar solutions.

There are many reference architectures available. Some align to specific applications and are provided by the applications vendors. Others can be used for completely custom solutions and where a variety of applications exist.

A classic reference architecture that could be relevant in our supply chain optimization example includes online transaction processing (OLTP) applications and a custom data warehouse and data marts. We might determine that we can build a viable solution by gathering data using batch feeds from financial, supply chain, human resources (HR), and customer relationship management (CRM) systems into an enterprise data warehouse. Business intelligence, machine learning, and other AI tools could be used to manipulate the data stored in the enterprise data warehouse or in data marts and deliver the information that we need.

As the data is sourced from only transactional systems in this architecture, all of it resides in tables. Hence, this architecture is comprised of relational databases for data management and the data is sourced from OLTP systems using data extraction, transformation, and loading (ETL) tools.

The architecture is illustrated in Figure 5-5.

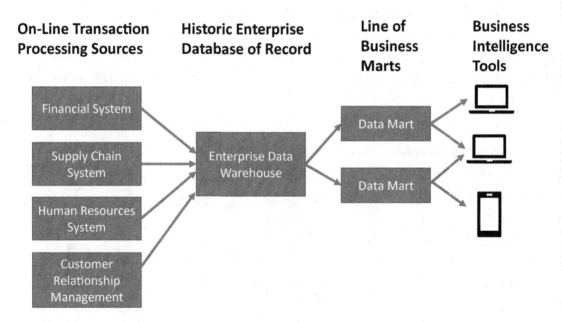

Figure 5-5. *Typical OLTP applications and data warehouse footprint*

In our supply chain optimization example, gathering data from these transactional data sources, building reports and dashboards, and incorporating machine learning and AI to make predictions might be all that is needed to solve the organization's problems. In that situation, the architecture shown in Figure 5-5 would suffice.

If there is a need to extend the data sources to Internet-of-Things (IoT) devices that produce streaming data and enable near real-time processing of the data, additional components must be introduced into the architecture. These would include components, such as the IoT edge devices themselves, IoT gateways, IoT hubs, streaming analytics engines, in-memory data preparation and training tools, and a data lake serving as an added data management system.

A typical reference architecture that includes the earlier mentioned OLTP applications and adds the IoT devices is illustrated in Figure 5-6. The portions of the architecture where data is manipulated in batch (the batch layer) and in near real time (the speed layer) are also delineated.

In good architecture design, form follows function. The type of architecture chosen is driven by the data required in the defined solution, the types of data sources and frequency of sourcing, operations that are performed upon the data, and how the data and information must be presented.

In our supply chain optimization example, if we plan to use data from IoT edge devices to report on the location and volume of the supplies and stream the data in near real time, we might choose to analyze this data at the edge (in the devices), along the data path, and/or in a data lake. Thus, the architecture that we would choose would likely resemble that shown in Figure 5-6.

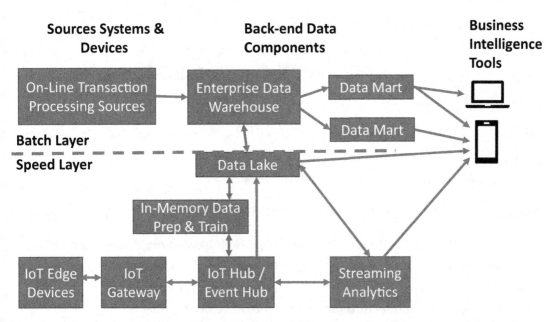

Figure 5-6. *Typical footprint with IoT devices as streaming data sources*

So far, we have approached the reference architecture at a conceptual level. What follows next is a more detailed evaluation of individual components available from cloud providers and other vendors. In many organizations, there are standards established defining many of these components to take advantage of skills already present in the organization and/or previous experience. Sometimes, a project such as this one might cause the organization to reevaluate some or all the component choices previously made (especially if there is some dissatisfaction with previous technologies selected).

In the supply chain optimization example, the organization has decided that it wants to employ AI to predict future supply chain shortages. When embarking on these types of projects, the authors have found that organizations sometimes already have data scientists using existing machine learning and AI footprints. However, we have also frequently observed that organizations must hire new data scientists to take part in new projects due to limited skills or limited bandwidth available from those already onboard.

If faced with hiring new data science talent, it is useful to understand that there are a variety of deep learning and AI frameworks and toolkits available. Some popular examples include TensorFlow, PyTorch, and cognitive toolkits from the cloud vendors. Data scientists will very often have a strong preference to use one of these offerings based on their training. They usually also have a favorite programming language in mind. Thus, the talent hired can impact the specific components that are defined in the future state architecture.

Prototype and Solution Evaluation

Prototype development, determining alignment of the prototype with the desired solution, and evolving the organization's architecture are not usually accomplished in a single sequential process. At each step in the incremental building process, a best practice is to have developers, key stakeholders, and frontline workers provide feedback and input into the direction of the effort. These reviews should take place frequently, typically every week or two.

As with the Design Thinking methodology that we covered in previous chapters, our intent in the prototype creation stage is to fail fast by quickly identifying mandated changes and fail forward continuing to improve the likelihood of solution success. The ongoing engagement of this group also serves to keep everyone up to date as to the progress being made and can help build a feeling of collaborative ownership for the project.

There is a chance that prototype development will uncover that the envisioned solution is untenable. Possible reasons for this conclusion include

- A lack of satisfaction with the prototype

- A growing concern about eventual cost of a solution

- A lack of belief in solution business benefits

- Changing business conditions and requirements that are placing more emphasis on solving other problems

- Turnover in organization sponsorships

- A growing concern about the risk of solution success (especially among sponsors)

- A realization that implementation and user skills are lacking in the organization

- Discovery of major skills gaps in implementation partners determined vital to success

If the problem that the organization needs to focus on changes, it is time to revisit the problems that were identified in the Design Thinking workshop. It is possible that this new more important problem was also explored. If not, another Design Thinking workshop should be held to uncover more information about the new problem and define new potential solutions.

If the problem that we focused on is still considered to be the right one to solve but the selected solution no longer appears to be viable, we should revisit the other solutions proposed during the Design Thinking workshop. We might find a better path to follow there.

We might also determine that the solution could be viable but needs an adjustment. This can be especially true if new stakeholders enter the picture, skills gaps are determined, and/or cost containment becomes an overriding concern. Here, the nature and scope of the proposed solution and the envisioned project to build and deploy it should be reevaluated.

Summary

In this chapter, we explored how to use the problem space and solution space information that was gathered in the earlier Design Thinking workshop to create a solution prototype comprised of software and/or AI technology components. We emphasized doing just enough during this stage of development to prove the viability of the defined solution.

You should now understand these:

- Approaches used in SDLC prototyping

- Steps in rapid building and testing of user interface prototypes

- When to consider applications vs. an entirely custom-built solution

- How to leverage reference architectures

- Evaluating the success of prototypes and possible reasons to revisit the solution

We also described how using these techniques and reference architectures could be applied in the supply chain optimization example. These illustrations should help you see how a software and AI project can become a natural outcome of a Design Thinking workshop and help you understand the value that the earlier workshop provides.

In the next chapter, we move beyond prototype development with a focus on what should be done after the prototype proves to be successful. In many organizations, a full-fledged project must be sold to senior executives to gain needed funding. We'll describe how to do that. We'll also explore moving the envisioned solution into the production development stage once project approval is gained.

CHAPTER 6

Production Development

Up to this point, the funding for the Design Thinking workshop and prototype development has probably come from monies set aside within normal business planning and technology evaluation budgets. Once a solution prototype is determined to be successful, additional monies must often be procured to bring the solution into production.

It is usually senior executives within the organization who must assess the value in funding the full build out of the solution. They need to be convinced of the potential payback and technical viability of the proposed solution prior to any required additional monies being allocated.

As the project moves toward production, additional technology investments and investments in skills development or hiring might be necessary. Established approaches within the organization for moving software and AI projects through development and into production are usually followed. The choices that are made will impact timelines and the potential risk to project success.

In this chapter, we focus on describing how to gain consensus on funding and an approach to development that has gained much popularity. The chapter contains the following major sections:

- Selling the project

- Development philosophy and DevOps

- Summary

Selling the Project

We first explored some of the key stakeholders who would be interested in solving the defined problem during the Design Thinking workshop (see Chapter 3). We created proto-personas for a few of these individuals. Before gathering the information needed to put together our request for funding, we should revisit these proto-personas and list

R. Stackowiak and T. Kelly, *Design Thinking in Software and AI Projects*

of stakeholders. While this earlier work will be of value now, some of the stakeholders we identified might have left the organization. New ones might have joined or taken on a more significant role.

Of course, now that we have a successful prototype, we should have a much better idea as to who will benefit from the solution. We should revisit our assumptions about who will be interested in funding the project and reevaluate the power structure in the organization. With an updated list of key decision-makers and influencers, we can evaluate how the successful prototype might influence their opinions regarding the viability of the solution.

Keep in mind that your various audiences will have different motivations driving their opinions. Executives will be mostly looking for the economic impact to their business. Frontline workers will judge project viability based on its impact to their job. Technical folks are likely to be highly supportive if they see that the potential project will drive new skills development, help them reconnect to the business, and gain a new source of funds. However, IT management might also be fearful of change if critical skills are lacking and are difficult to develop or hire from outside the organization. Use your sponsor(s) to help coach you through appropriate messaging for each group.

Once we understand their motivations and how the project's impact will align, we should have a better idea as to what will drive a decision to move beyond the prototype stage. In most projects, there is a standard set of information that must be provided. Here, we will assemble the key information that is needed into a presentation will be used when delivering the message that seeks funding for production development.

Gathering Needed Information

An extensive amount information must be gathered as a business case for bringing the solution into production is prepared. Detailed analysis and preparation of the following information will enable leadership to understand the scope of the effort:

- Projected costs of developing the production-quality solution

- Ongoing costs of maintaining the solution once it is put into production

- Projected financial and soft benefits accrued as the solution is deployed and adopted

- Timeline of development and rollout

- Timeline of costs and benefits accrued

- Risks to the project's success and mitigation steps

When considering the costs of development of the production-quality solution, development staff costs can be estimated by projecting the amount of time it will take software developers and/or data scientists to do their work. Also considered are costs associated with further skills development (such as training) if the organization is building the solution with internal resources.

The development team will need access to technology that can be scaled to mimic production-level workloads. Thus, the costs of underlying technology needed for development and costs of scaling cloud-based solutions or deploying additional technology resources should be included. The costs of full production scale-out, along with related ongoing support, should also be included in an estimate of costs that will accrue.

Reasonable estimates of the business benefits that will accrue as the solution rolls out into production are also made. Examples of where tangible benefits might come include

- Positive impact on revenue

- Cost avoidance and reductions in existing costs

- Creation of new business services adding value

- Improved flexibility in responding to changing customer and market demands

These benefits should be linked to the timelines for development and rollout while also noting the impacted business areas.

Note   The more detailed you can be in gathering costs and benefits, the better. A lot of this data will be summarized later when delivering the message that will be used in selling the project. However, since the CFO is often a very important evaluator of these projects, they will appreciate the detail behind the summary. They might be enlisted to help with the project's financial justification as they likely have standard practices and formulae in place for doing such evaluations within your organization. For example, they might use net present value (NPV) to account for the value of money over time in their computations. They might also prefer to evaluate a range of estimates from conservative to "best guess" to most optimistic.

Finally, we'll need to denote the risks to project success that we see along the way. This might seem at first as something that we want to avoid given that we are trying to sell the need for project funds. However, experienced senior executives know that there are risks in any project, especially where the project is truly innovative. They will want to know what those risks are and how the organization should mitigate them. The fact that you have researched this and can provide reasonable answers will go a long way in convincing executives that this is a viable solution.

Some of the typical risks often considered in these projects include

- Possible disruption of existing business processes

- Emerging competitive threats and timing of solution deployment

- Introduction of new technologies and algorithms to solve problems

- Complexity of technology, solution design, and scope

- Concerns about information privacy and liability that could be introduced

- Costs associated with the project

- Skills shortages in internal software development/data science staff and IT

- Skills shortages in technology partners

- Skills lacking among potential users of the solution

- Possible delays in rollout timing impacting the ability to achieve business benefit

Mitigation steps might include transition plans minimizing disruptions, more speedy delivery of portions of the solution in anticipation of competitive threats delivering more business value sooner, simplification of designs, proactive information security procedures, and skills development and/or hiring plans targeting various parts of the organization.

Given that you could encounter skills shortages in several areas, you might perform skills assessments during this information gathering stage. You should decide what major categories of skills are needed for key roles and specific skills required in each category. The assessment should include questions about how widespread the skills are in the organization. For example, skills ratings might range from none (rated as a "0") to very widespread (rated as a "5").

As an example, we assessed data science skills across the organization deploying the supply chain optimization example that we are using in this book. We determined that the major categories of skills and specific skills needed in each category are as follows:

- Data skills

    - Experience working with data from a variety of relational databases

    - Experience working with data from NoSQL databases and data lakes

    - Familiarity with third-party data sources that could prove useful

    - Data cleansing and data preparation experience

- Business skills

    - Demonstrated ability to probe for business requirements and use them to drive toward an impactful solution

    - Demonstrated ability to communicate well with business executives and frontline workers

- Math (modeling) skills

    - Experience with statistics and machine learning algorithms

    - Experience with unsupervised learning/AI algorithms

- Programming skills

    - Experience coding in Python

    - Experience coding in Java

    - Experience using ML/AI frameworks

    - Experience performing sprints and building containers as part of a DevOps team

The results of our assessment are illustrated in Figure 6-1.

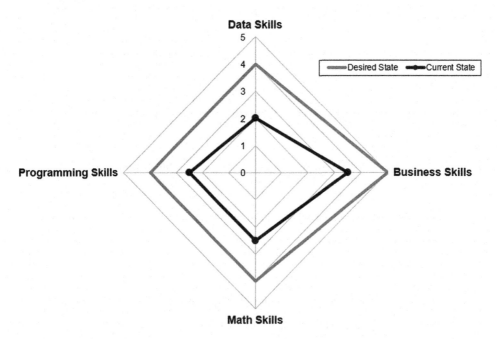

Figure 6-1. *Skills assessment for data science in the organization*

We see in Figure 6-1 that the current state plot of skills (inner line with points) does not match or exceed the desired future state plot (outer line) in any of the skills categories. This tells us that the organization needs to develop these skills internally, hire data scientists with these skills, and/or rely on consulting partners to fill this gap. It should be noted that by going through this exercise, we also have identified the skills that we expect the data scientists to be capable of and we can use those requirements in defining their job description.

The Selling Message

Though a tremendous amount of information and technical detail is usually gathered, it is more detailed than is needed or desired by key project funding decision-makers. This is usually especially true for the most senior executives who must support the effort. At this point, a presentation must be assembled that will help sell the project to this audience.

The presentation is often delivered by the key sponsor(s) and needs to be focused and short, delivering just the information that the audience cares about and needs. It should typically be 30 minutes in length or less. Our recommended presentation flow is as follows:

- A summary of the project recommendation including key benefits and funding needed

- An agenda slide that describes what is in the remainder of the presentation

- A summary of the business problem(s) solved and expected solution benefits

- A timeline summarizing key development and solution delivery milestones and attainment of benefits expected along the way

- A summary of technology elements to be included in the solution

- A discussion of risks to project success and how those will be mitigated

- Quotes from sponsors, frontline workers, and others backing the project

- A summary of next steps immediately after funding approval

You might wonder why we start the presentation with a summary. If the project is being sold at very senior levels, the executive(s) in the room could be interrupted by other business emergencies five minutes into the presentation. You will want to make sure that the presenter has made the point about the value of the project and what is being asked for in funding before this interruption occurs. If executives do need to leave the room, at least we have gotten their attention and should be able to reschedule the rest of the presentation sooner rather than later if needed.

To illustrate a typical presentation, we will revisit our supply chain optimization example used throughout this book. Our sample presentation consists of just eight slides.

Figure 6-2 pictures the initial slide summarizing the benefits and funding needed to bring the solution prototype into production. Noted here is an investment needed to improve management of the supply chain in a "lead" plant in the first year. The lead plant is the most technology advanced with many sensors and smart equipment already in place. Also noted is the additional revenue gained by making the initial investment along with similar figures provided for the second year when the solution is deployed across all plants and the supply chain can be optimized across them. A simple graph is shown to illustrate when positive ROI is likely to occur.

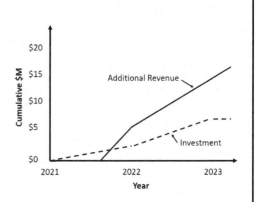

Figure 6-2. *Initial slide summarizing our funding request presentation*

The agenda slide follows. It serves an important role here as it lays out the scope of the content that follows in the presentation. The audience might want to skip to certain slides later as they might already understand some aspects of the project and the solution. They might also want to drill into more detail on certain topics. Presenting this slide now can give the presenter an early heads-up as to where the audience will want to focus and help keep topic discussions within the timeframe that is available.

The agenda slide for the supply chain optimization project presentation is illustrated in Figure 6-3.

Supply Chain Optimization Project:
Today's Agenda

- Business Drivers
- Project Phases
- Key Technologies
- Risk Mitigation
- Project Support
- Next Steps

Figure 6-3. *Agenda slide in our funding request presentation*

A description of the business problems that are going to be solved by the solution follows. For each business problem, the solution benefits and measurable goals are provided. In the supply chain optimization project, the primary goal is to minimize out-of-stock parts and components. A secondary goal is to eliminate wasted inventory in the plants.

These benefits and goals are shown in the slide pictured in Figure 6-4.

Supply Chain Optimization Business Drivers

Minimize out-of-stock parts and components	Eliminate wasted inventory
Achieve higher revenue by manufacturing quantities needed to meet demand	Ensure all inventory on hand is necessary and used
Minimize idle manufacturing equipment in plants	Ensure all needed inventory is delivered just-in-time whenever possible
Measurable Goals	**Measurable Goals**
Increase revenue attributable to improved manufacturing processes in our most advanced plant by at least $5 million in the first year	Reduction in inventory value write-offs by 15 percent
Modernize other plants and optimize production across all facilities improving overall revenue by at least $10 million per year	Free up inventory floor space in factories by 20 percent enabling more manufacturing equipment to be put in place

Figure 6-4. *Summary slide of business problems solved and solution benefits*

The audience will want to see a simplified view of major project milestones to understand major phases and their timing. Senior executives will also want to understand how quickly they can expect tangible results from the project.

Figure 6-5 presents a timeline to show exactly that. On the timeline, there is an indication that the first positive ROI will occur in the second half of 2021 (even before the solution is fully deployed in the first plant). During the second half of 2022, it will be possible to begin to rationalize the supply chain across all the plants. The project will be fully deployed not long after the end of 2022.

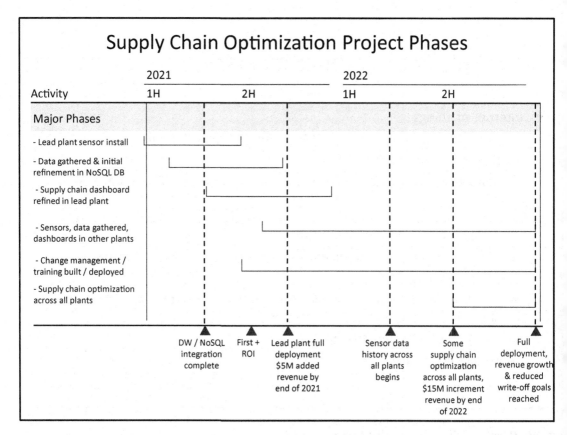

Figure 6-5. *Project timeline and accrued benefits expected*

The next slide describes key technology elements in the solution. Though IT organizations often want to provide a lot more detail here and possibly include architecture diagrams, that could lead to the least interesting and most confusing discussion for many in the audience.

On this slide, there is simply a list highlighting some of the key technology elements as shown in Figure 6-6. Diagrams of the current state and future state architecture are best left in an optional slide portion of the presentation (e.g., placed in a supplemental section) and used with more technology-oriented audiences.

Supply Chain Optimization Key Technologies

- Internet of Things
  - Devices & sensors monitoring manufacturing equipment, supplies
- Machine Learning and AI
  - Cloud-based tools and frameworks used to analyze and predict shortages and oversupply
  - Cloud-based business intelligence tools delivering dashboards to executives, management, and front-line workers
  - Automated alerts to management, front-line workers, suppliers, distributors
- Data Management
  - Cloud-based NoSQL and relational data management solutions appropriate for streaming and transactional data sources
- Reliable and Secure Networking
  - Linking all the above

Figure 6-6. *Technology elements summary*

Of important consideration by most executive audiences are the risks that the project will introduce. They especially want to hear of plans regarding how to overcome significant risks through mitigation efforts.

The slide illustrated in Figure 6-7 is intended to answer many of the likely questions that the audience has in a proactive manner. It lists the risks and summarizes the mitigation effort for each. Of course, the presenter will provide more detailed explanations of the mitigation efforts as needed.

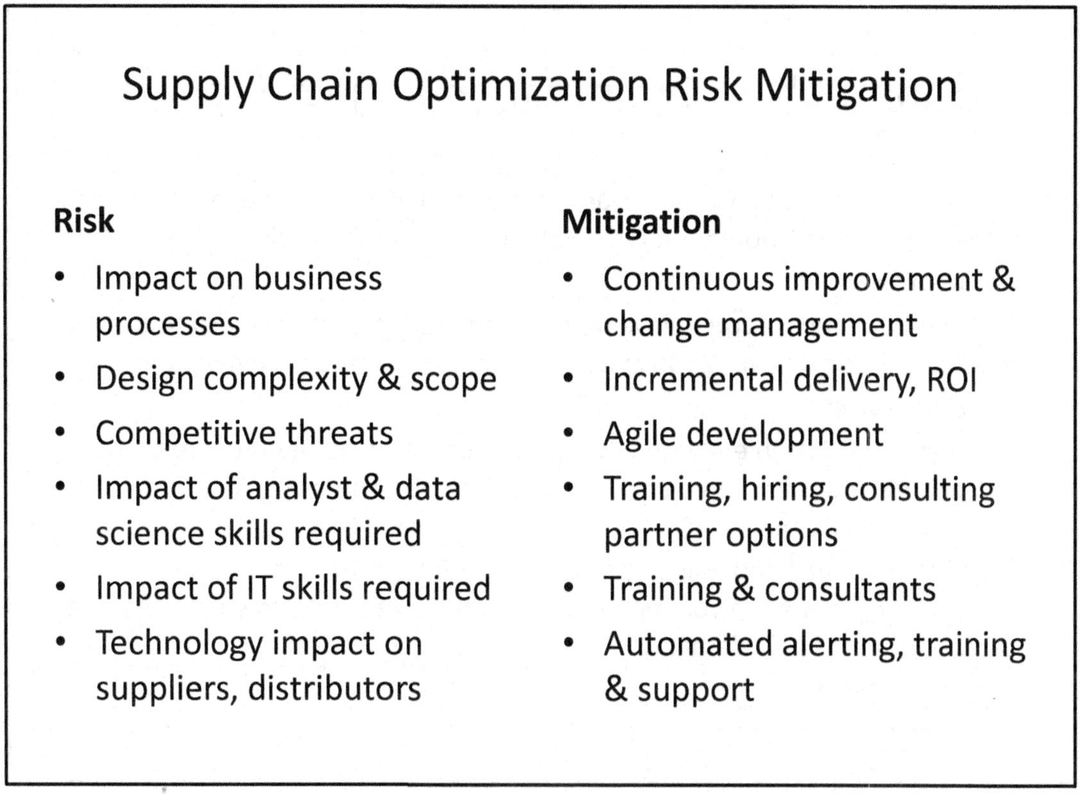

Supply Chain Optimization Risk Mitigation

Risk	Mitigation
• Impact on business processes	• Continuous improvement & change management
• Design complexity & scope	• Incremental delivery, ROI
• Competitive threats	• Agile development
• Impact of analyst & data science skills required	• Training, hiring, consulting partner options
• Impact of IT skills required	• Training & consultants
• Technology impact on suppliers, distributors	• Automated alerting, training & support

Figure 6-7. *Project risks and mitigation*

You might think that quotes from individuals supporting the project are superfluous. We have found them useful in illustrating widespread support within an organization and in validating some of the information previously presented.

We show some examples of quotes from important individuals impacted by the supply chain optimization project in the slide pictured in Figure 6-8.

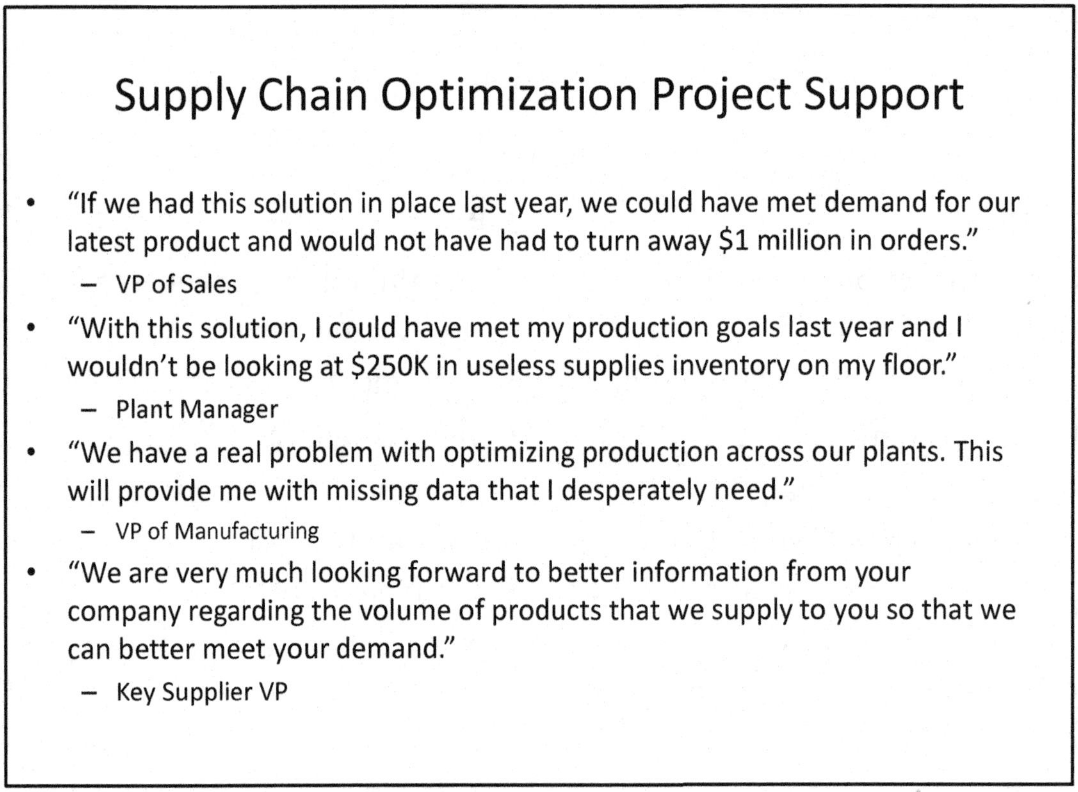

Supply Chain Optimization Project Support

- "If we had this solution in place last year, we could have met demand for our latest product and would not have had to turn away $1 million in orders."
  - VP of Sales
- "With this solution, I could have met my production goals last year and I wouldn't be looking at $250K in useless supplies inventory on my floor."
  - Plant Manager
- "We have a real problem with optimizing production across our plants. This will provide me with missing data that I desperately need."
  - VP of Manufacturing
- "We are very much looking forward to better information from your company regarding the volume of products that we supply to you so that we can better meet your demand."
  - Key Supplier VP

Figure 6-8. *Supporting quotes from key stakeholders*

Note   To get impactful quotes to be used in this presentation, we suggest interviewing a wide array of people who will see benefits in the project being deployed. You might need to probe a bit to get financial impact numbers, but these are often the most effective quotes to use.

Your audience will want to know what comes next if the monies being asked for in funding are approved. This final slide in the presentation outlines some immediate next steps at a high level (with additional detail verbally provided by the presenter). It is pictured in Figure 6-9.

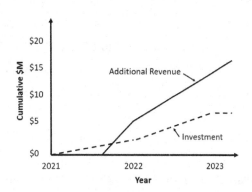

Supply Chain Optimization Next Steps

- Funding approval for the project
  - $2M in first year
  - $5M in second year
- Assemble project team
- Refine change management plan for organization
- Transition from prototype development to production development and deployment

Figure 6-9. *Summary of next steps*

It is to be expected that more detailed questions will be asked during the presentation. That is when having the detailed information that was gathered previously will come in handy. Having some additional detailed slides ready, just in case they are needed, is always a good idea.

Development Philosophy and DevOps

In many organizations, production development can begin shortly after funding is approved. The development methodology used in your organization is likely to be either a traditional waterfall approach or a modern DevOps approach. Regardless of the approach that is used, the techniques described previously in this book for problem identification, solution definition, prototype creation, and selling the project should prove to be extremely useful in reaching the production development stage.

Note   Sometimes, organizations that are developing software and AI solutions considered to provide competitive business advantage choose to designate multiple development teams to work in parallel, each racing to solve the same problem. Teams might choose to develop using different approaches and/or underlying technologies and applications adaptation strategies. The competing solutions are usually evaluated for their viability based on multiple factors such as how well they solve the problem, comparative costs, usability, scalability, complexity, risk, and time to production. A solution is selected that best meets the evaluation criteria factors deemed most important to the organization.

The traditional waterfall approach is defined by a sequence of steps. The approach begins with the gathering of requirements (which we did during the Design Thinking workshop) and then proceeds through design (which we started during our prototype creation), implementation (the production software/AI development step), testing and verification of the code, and finally deployment. These steps are illustrated in Figure 6-10.

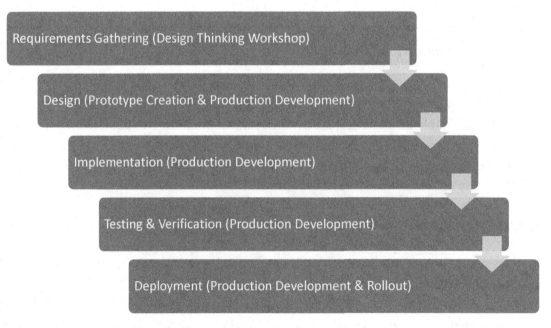

Figure 6-10. *Waterfall approach process flow*

The development, testing and verification, and deployment steps are often tracked through project management tools that indicate achievement of milestones. The model within the project management tool typically shows parallel development efforts (where possible) and is used to determine critical paths to the solution deployment.

Organizations relying on the waterfall development approach often have large development teams engaged. The time to deployment of the solution can be lengthy. Deployment is usually the first time that the users can see how the production solution functions.

A modern DevOps approach enables frequent incremental reviews during solution development. You might have assumed that putting together a timeline with major milestones (like was done to sell the need for funding) could preclude a DevOps approach during this phase of development. To the contrary, we believe that the DevOps process has proven that it can support fast movement toward such major milestones in software development projects and is therefore extremely useful.

In organizations where DevOps is adopted, software development usually occurs in incremental sprints of two to three weeks in length. Small cross-functional teams are assembled to take part in the sprints. Teams often work in parallel and sprints occur back to back; thus, the code development process is often described as following a model of continuous integration and continuous deployment (CI/CD).

The continuous process begins by planning to build specific capabilities or features in the proposed application. The earlier prototype development that we described in Chapter 5 provides important input regarding what is needed in the application. The team leader and team members should understand the solution definition first provided in the Design Thinking workshop and subsequently fine-tuned. Generally, capabilities considered to be the most important to providing the solution (or those that are prerequisites for providing key functionality) are tackled first.

Capabilities are quickly built in software and then compiled into executables. They are tested using relevant data files and deployed when ready. Executables are run for a short time and monitored. Success rates of incremental builds are tracked to understand the delivery performance of the team. Lessons are learned from the execution and monitoring, and then subsequent sprints are planned and/or modified.

Figure 6-11 illustrates the typical continuous DevOps process flow as a closed loop.

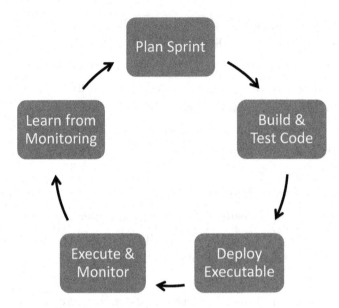

Figure 6-11. *DevOps process flow*

Input from intended users of the solution is critical throughout the DevOps process so they are sometimes included as members of the cross-functional teams. Especially valuable is input from the same individuals who took part in the Design Thinking workshop and prototype development evaluation as they can help to keep development focused on delivering a viable solution. As capabilities are delivered that begin to demonstrate how the solution will function, the users can evaluate them and suggest what subsequent sprints must focus on. They can also communicate back to stakeholders and executives regarding progress that is being made in solving the business problem.

Today, a popular approach in CI/CD involves deploying application code in the form of microservices. Each microservice performs a distinct task and communicates with other microservices through APIs. The trade-offs and value of using this approach were still much debated when this book was published.

Building microservices is a beneficial approach to application development in that they are independently scalable, can be deployed in a fault-tolerant manner, and can be reused by multiple applications. They can be written or rewritten in a variety of languages and not impact the overall application integrity.

However, microservices also introduce a need for better documentation and communication among development teams. They can introduce non-optimal performance challenges and are often more complex and costly to operate and maintain.

There are several tools that help to enable successful development efforts using a DevOps approach. Some of the tools needed include

- Collaborative sprint planning and tracking tools

- A repository for sharing code and data files

- Containers and orchestration tools

- Pipelines used in building, testing, and deploying code

- Test planning tools

Machine learning and AI projects add the need to focus on management of data during sprints. Data orchestration and cleansing tools are added to the list of technologies important for successful development. Since changes in real-world conditions can also impact results and a variety of CPUs and GPUs are often tested, versioning capabilities are also an essential part of the toolkit.

Cloud-based vendors are recognizing the need for services to address these additional requirements in machine learning and AI projects. For example, Microsoft's Azure ML Service provides a framework for running experiments, managing pipelines, assigning compute, managing models and images (containers), and deploying the solutions.

Note   Moving to a DevOps style of development from a traditional waterfall approach requires a significant shift in the procedures, tools utilized, and the size, makeup, and management of the teams. As DevOps is a popular topic these days, there are hundreds of books, whitepapers, and documentation describing techniques and best practices in much more detail than we covered in this chapter. Our goal here was to simply describe DevOps in the context of moving the defined solution's development effort forward.

Summary

In this chapter, we provided guidance regarding moving from prototype creation into production development. We also noted how information gathered in the earlier Design Thinking workshop impacted the following:

- Selling the project, including gathering the right information and putting it together in a message used to request funding

- Moving to development using a traditional waterfall approach or using a continuous integration and continuous development approach (modern DevOps), including how these techniques fit into software and AI projects

You should now understand how to formulate a message that will fund the solution that was first identified in the Design Thinking workshop and further developed as a prototype. You should also understand differences between the traditional waterfall development approach and the modern DevOps approach as well as some of the possible trade-offs to consider.

In the next and final chapter, we cover techniques for planning the rollout of the technology solution, change management needed to get the entire organization ready, and how to determine whether the project is successful. We will conclude the book with some thoughts about what likely will occur after the production rollout stage is complete.

CHAPTER 7

Production Rollout

This chapter focuses on the rollout of a project's solution into production. We begin by discussing operationalization considerations in software and AI projects. We explore the typical roles and key activities of individuals. We then describe some of the operational procedures prior to and during limited production with the intent of having them completely implemented when reaching full production.

A successful rollout also requires careful and well-planned change management to assure wide adoption and deliver needed levels of service and support. So, we next discuss how we already created a strong change management foundation during the earlier stages previously covered in this book and the additional change management tasks that are particularly relevant to successful rollout of the production solution.

As our solution achieves production status, we should assess how successful the deployed solution is and use what we learn in the assessment to make corrections as needed. We should also assess the entire process used to reach this point and use the knowledge that we gained to improve how we go about identifying and solving problems in the future.

Finally, in addition to summarizing the chapter, we discuss what you should have learned by reading this book. We also call attention to the circular nature of the approach that we covered and its key stages.

Thus, this chapter contains the following major sections:

- Operationalizing the solution

- Change management considerations

- Assessing project success

- Summary

© Robert Stackowiak and Tracey Kelly 2020
R. Stackowiak and T. Kelly, *Design Thinking in Software and AI Projects*

Operationalizing the Solution

At the point that a solution is deemed ready for more widespread use and adoption, we must consider what it will take to make this possible. Many organizations identify and begin to solve operational challenges during their DevOps development cycles or when they deliver a limited production environment prior to moving into full production. As part of such efforts, they identify critical tasks and procedures that need to be put into place to deliver needed levels of service and support.

When we earlier put together the message used to sell the project to senior executives, we estimated staffing costs required to bring the solution into production. As we begin monitoring the incremental development and production efforts, we should uncover more information about who these key individuals are and the tasks that they must perform. We might also need to evaluate additional staffing needed to perform tasks that we had not earlier anticipated. A typical approach used during these evaluations is to identify who is responsible (R), accountable (A), consulted (C), and/or informed (I) for a variety of tasks (often referred to as RACI).

For example, the key activities identified for cloud-based PaaS deployment of software and AI solutions could include day-to-day operations, monitoring the solution, application and platform change management, application release management, performance tuning, and data protection. The people we might focus on in our evaluation include stakeholders and frontline workers, analysts and data scientists, cloud administrators, data administrators, developers, and IT managers.

A RACI diagram is used to indicate the key activities for this group of people. An illustration is provided in Figure 7-1.

Activity	Stakeholder, Frontline Worker	Analyst / Data Scientist	Cloud Platform Administrator	Data Administrator	Solution Developer	IT Manager
Day to day operations	I		R			A
Platform & solution monitoring	I	I	R			A
Platform change management	I	I	R	C / R	R	A
Application release management	C	R	I	I	R	A / I
Performance optimization	C	C	R	R	R / C / I	A
Data protection	C	R / C / I	C	R		A

Figure 7-1. *Typical RACI diagram defining roles for software and AI operationalization*

The activities and people designated in RACI diagrams are influenced by the type of technology infrastructure utilized in the production deployment. For instance, a more extensive list of IT-related activities and staff would be required for deployment of an on-premise solution than that which we denoted for a cloud-based PaaS deployment. We would need to add systems administrators, storage administrators, network administrators, and data center managers to the list of critical staff. Activities such as infrastructure configuration, software patching, hardware and software updates, and data center infrastructure coordination and planning would be added.

In our supply chain optimization example that we have referenced in this book, we also indicated a need to deploy intelligent devices to track supplies and their utilization in the manufacturing plants. A typical RACI diagram focused on IoT edge deployment is shown in Figure 7-2. Here, we designate day-to-day operations, device monitoring, device maintenance, device software releases, network monitoring (including within plants), and device protection as key activities. People included in this evaluation include stakeholders and frontline workers, analysts and data scientists, device administrators, device software developers, and plant managers.

Activity	Stakeholder, Frontline Worker	Analyst / Data Scientist	Device Administrator	Network Administrator	Device Software Developer	Plant Manager
Day to day operations	I		R	R		A
Device monitoring			R	I / R		A
Device maintenance	I	I	R	I	C / I	A
Device software releases	C	R / I	I	I	R	A / I
Network monitoring	C	C / I	I	R	C / I	I
Device protection	C	I	R	R	R / I	A

Figure 7-2. *Typical RACI diagram defining roles where IoT devices deployed*

RACI diagrams can also be extended to illustrate the delivery of specific levels of service and denote the individuals and their responsibilities in delivering them. Examples of areas of service-level focus include resource availability (and related technical implementations such as high availability and disaster recovery) and infrastructure security (including infrastructure, software, and data security).

Levels of detail provided within these diagrams can also vary. Some organizations choose to build RACI diagrams for each of the major activities that they identify and then break those activities into detailed tasks for which they also provide RACI diagrams.

Our next step is to document the procedures that are to be put into place to perform required tasks. The procedures are defined by considering previous procedures already in place within the organization, knowledge gained in prototyping the solution, and previous experience obtained by scaling other prototypes into full production.

A sample list of some of the procedures that would likely be defined to enable successful rollout and ongoing support of the example supply chain optimization solution include

- Application deployment and updates

- Auditing of devices and infrastructure

- Business continuity and disaster recovery

- Cloud and/or IT infrastructure policy

- Communications access to devices, equipment, and infrastructure software and data

- Data exchange policies and standards

- Help desk support

- Incident management and remediation

- Networking and device management, monitoring, and maintenance

- Networking and device standards for the organization

- Physical access to equipment in data centers and plants

- Security policies

The procedures are generally refined and tested during DevOps cycles or during a limited early production phase of deployment. Scalability testing likely also occurs during this time by simulating workloads and situations that will be likely when the solution is in full production.

Note   AI projects require additional governance procedures be put into place as the accuracy of models often changes over time. Retesting of models leveraging more recent data and evaluations of the results of actions that have been taken should occur at regular intervals to determine when the models and actions need to be tweaked.

Change Management Considerations

Innovative software and AI projects, by definition, drive change. Managing change is an important aspect of assuring successful rollout of such projects. Best practices have been documented by numerous people and organizations who have expertise in change management over the past 70 years. Examples of such methodologies that gained a popular following include those defined by Kotter, Lewin, McKinsey, and Prosci.

There is much shared in common by these approaches. We believe that when all these approaches are considered, it is evident that change management needs to focus on the following tasks:

- Gaining support that change is needed to solve the problem

- Gaining agreement that the envisioned change will solve the problem

- Developing talents and skills needed to build, deploy, manage, and use the solution

- Modifying organizational constructs and shifting responsible individuals where needed

- Positively reinforcing those who successfully utilize the solution

The Design Thinking workshop is a critical early piece of the change management process. Remember that we gained support that change was needed and formulated a vision of the potential solution during the workshop. During the subsequent building of the prototype and then development of the solution, we began developing skills needed for successful deployment and management.

As we go into production, we must revisit the skills present in our frontline workers and among the management who will use the solution. If there are skills gaps, we will need to implement a training and rollout plan that closes the gaps and monitor success in utilization of the solution. As part of this effort, a popular best practice is to identify those with early expertise and assign them to act as mentors for those less experienced during the rollout.

Note   The skills that are evaluated for frontline workers and management likely include business skills as well as technology utilization skills. In our supply chain optimization example, important business skills required might include those related to inventory management, supply chain planning, demand planning, transportation planning, order management, manufacturing, contracting, and/or financial management.

During the rollout, one of our goals is to continue to build solution utilization momentum. Senior management can help drive positive momentum by offering meaningful rewards and recognition to those successfully applying the solution. Those who resist change should be provided with additional guidance and training, and it should be made clear that they need to adapt and utilize the solution if they are to be viewed as a positive contributor to the business.

Figure 7-3 illustrates when the key change management tasks that we denoted are initiated. We use this diagram to show when the tasks are executed relative to the Design Thinking workshop, prototype development, production development, and production rollout stages that are described in this book.

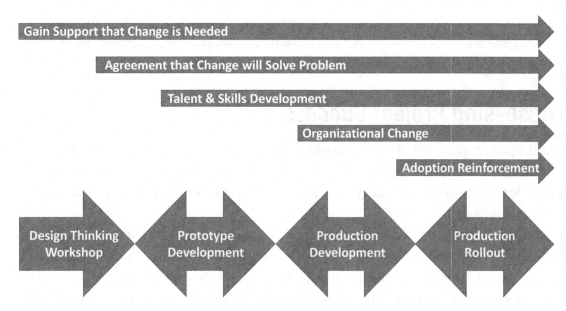

Figure 7-3. *Change management applied to key stages described in this book*

You probably noticed that we illustrated many of the stages by using arrows that point in both directions. As many of these projects tend to evolve over time and roadblocks to success can emerge, there is sometimes a need to revisit earlier stages.

We believe that initiating change management steps as early as possible within the stages will result in more well-thought-out steps and greater maturation over time. As a result, the steps will have a greater positive impact on the organization.

Some experts suggest developing a communications plan during the production rollout stage. We believe that it is important to have ongoing communications procedures defined throughout each of the stages to convey changing project plans, project status, and solution focus. During production rollout, the communications plan should be fine-tuned with focus on the arrival of the solution for general use as well as its impact upon the broader organization.

We can utilize the earlier identified sponsors to assist in our communications to frontline workers during production rollout. We might also enlist additional key managers to support our communications efforts and help broaden the solution adoption.

No doubt, there will be some resistance to the changes that occur. We should have a plan ready to address such resistance, whether the resistance comes from some in management or frontline workers. Such resistance to adoption is sometimes uncovered as we assess the project's success.

Assessing Project Success

As the project solution rolls out, it should be continually assessed as to whether it is addressing the business problem that it was meant to solve. Doing so is important if you hope to gain momentum leading to widespread adoption of the solution beyond a core group of believers.

Geoffrey Moore described the challenges in gaining adoption of highly innovative solutions in his book *Crossing the Chasm*. It is interesting to note that in 1991, when he wrote the book, Moore identified AI as one such technology that had failed to gain wide adoption and was seemingly stalled. As you probably realize, the status of AI adoption changed significantly over the past decade when languages, tools, and frameworks emerged aiding its development and usage. The number of trained and skilled individuals capable of using such tools also exploded, and they were enabled by the widespread availability of cloud-based resources and compute power.

Moore pointed out that a technology adoption life cycle can be defined in discrete phases. He described people and organizations leading adoption within these phases as innovators, early adopters, an early majority, a late majority, and laggards. Peak adoption occurs during the early and late majority phases.

A goal of most software and AI projects is to have the production solution gain usage beyond the groups of innovators and early adopters within the organization. A fair and balanced assessment that looks at the state of the project and how it has evolved along the way should be undertaken.

Some of the questions that should be asked during the assessment include

- Did the solution deliverables match business requirements and solve the defined problem? If not, why not?

- Is adoption of the solution by frontline workers and management growing and is the predicted business value being delivered?

- Were project milestones met on time? If not, why not?

- Did prototype development transition smoothly into production development and deployment? If not, why not?

- Was the original budget for the project accurate? If not, why not?

- Were skills found wanting, developed along the way, or are they still in short supply (with internal organizations and/or partners constrained in providing the right people)?

- Were quality assessment practices put into place and did they improve the solution? How?

- Were technical operations and change management programs adequately planned for and successfully executed?

It should be possible to claim success if the answers to these previous questions are of a positive nature.

Note   If there are many issues, and especially if the business benefits are unclear or not as promised, you have more work to do on the solution. You cannot expect to see widespread adoption of a badly flawed solution or because of a poor rollout. If changes are determined to be necessary, it is time to have candid discussions with sponsors and frontline workers about the shortcomings that they see. The solution's design, development, and/or rollout plan should be changed appropriately.

When you do find responses of a positive nature during the assessment, be sure to also gather endorsements from key executives, stakeholders, and frontline workers, data regarding solution adoption related to the success, and the ongoing measurable business impact attributable to the solution. All this information should be included in reports and presentations regarding the results of the project and should prove valuable in convincing skeptics within your organization.

Some might argue that software and AI projects are never complete as continual improvements will occur and question whether there will ever be a right time to present this information. We believe that when adoption reaches a point where stakeholders and frontline workers attest that the solution is delivering the significant business results that were hoped for, that is a great time to present this content.

When you become confident in the project's success, you should share your findings with executives and key sponsors and highlight the following:

- Summarize the business results attributable to the problem's solution and the early feedback obtained.

- Provide an actual timeline of how the project progressed and came into production.

- Describe challenges that occurred during development and rollout and how they were overcome.

- Describe the important lessons learned.

- Describe how the scope of the solution might have been limited (especially if there are deferred modification requests, next steps identified in responding to these requests, and additional funding needed).

You can use this as an opportunity to point out that a key to assuring success of the project was the Design Thinking workshop at the beginning. You might gain new sponsors for future Design Thinking workshops and ensure that it becomes part of the problem-solving methodology present in your organization moving forward.

Summary

In this chapter, we described some of the important actions that should be taken during production rollout including

- Operationalizing the solution by defining key activities, steps, and procedures for people in various roles

- Considering the role of change management during the rollout stage with an added emphasis on reaching a broader community

- Assessing the success of the project using a defined set of questions, acting when needed to improve the solution, and using the responses to report results to senior executives and sponsors

If there was a bad miss in what was delivered in the project, a Design Thinking workshop might be held at this point to revisit the problem definition and solution. If the project proves successful, this is a great time to make sure that the workshop becomes part of the organization's problem identification and solution development methodology going forward.

Thus, we have come full circle in the book. A diagram illustrating the circular nature of traversing the key stages that were covered, including where Design Thinking workshops fit, is illustrated in Figure 7-4. Though we might need to revisit earlier stages within a cycle, as we gain experience using this approach, it becomes a repeatable engine for uncovering and solving problems.

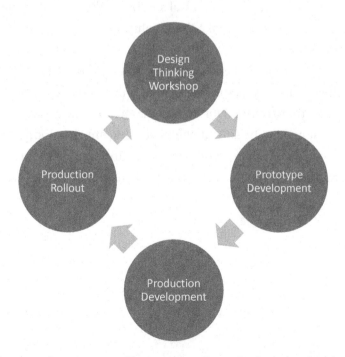

Figure 7-4. *The circular nature of key stages described in this book*

As we reach the end of this book, you should now have gained an understanding of this entire process including

- What Design Thinking is (including its history and common methodologies)

- How to prepare for a Design Thinking workshop

- Problem definition methods and tools used in the Design Thinking workshop

- Solution definition methods and tools used in the Design Thinking workshop

- How prototype creation is driven using information gathered in the workshop

- How to move from prototype development to production development

- How to operationalize the production solution and claiming success

Our hope is that this book provided you with guidance on how to identify problems in your organization and determine potential solutions. We also hope that it provided some practical thoughts on how to make these solutions real as you move beyond the Design Thinking workshop.

As a final thought, we would like to share this. Though software and AI proponents sometimes view the technology as something that only needs to be implemented to prove its value, it is far more optimal for an organization to understand the business problems present that need to be solved before starting any development efforts.

It is our hope that you now agree and can see the tremendous value in adopting a Design Thinking approach as part of your project development life cycle.

Sources

Books and Printed Sources

Arbinger Institute. *The Outward Mindset: Seeing Beyond Ourselves*. Oakland, CA: Berrett-Koehler Publishers, 2016.

Buzan, Tony & Raymond Keene. *Buzan's Book of Genius*. London: Stanley Paul, 1994.

Denscombe, Martyn. *The Good Research Guide*. Maidenhead, Berkshire, England: Open University Press/McGraw Hill, 1998 & 2014.

Dweck, Carol. *Mindset*. New York, NY: Random House, 2006.

Gelb, Michael J. *How to Think Like Leonardo da Vinci: Seven Steps to Genius Every Day*. New York, NY: Dell, 2000.

Isaacson, Walter. *Leonardo da Vinci*. New York, NY: Simon & Schuster, 2017.

Knapp, Jake, J. Zeratsky, B. Kowitz. *Sprint: How to Solve Big Problems and Test New Ideas in Just Five Days*. New York, NY: Simon & Schuster, 2016.

Laney, Douglas (Gartner, Inc.). *Infonomics*. New York, NY: Bibliomotion, Inc., 2018.

Lewrick, Michael, P. Link, L. Leifer. *The Design Thinking Playbook*. Hoboken, NJ: John Wiley & Sons, 2018.

Maxwell, John C. *Failing Forward: Turning Mistakes into Stepping Stones for Success*. Nashville, TN: Thomas Nelson Publishers, 2007.

Miller, Robert B. & Stephen E. Heiman. *Strategic Selling*. New York, NY: William Morrow and Company, 1985.

Moore, Geoffrey A. *Crossing the Chasm*. New York, NY: Harper Business, 1991.

Mueller-Roterberg, Christian. *Handbook of Design Thinking*. Independently published, 2018.

Osterwalder, Alexander & Yves Pigneur. *Business Model Generation: A Handbook for Visionaries, Game Changers, and Challengers*. Hoboken, NJ: John Wiley and Sons, 2010.

Stackowiak, Robert. *Azure Internet of Things Revealed: Architecture and Fundamentals*. New York, NY: Apress (Springer Media), 2019.

Stackowiak, Robert, A Licht, V Mantha, and L Nagode. *Big Data and The Internet of Things: Enterprise Architecture for a New Age.* New York, NY: Apress (Springer Media), 2015.

Stackowiak, Robert, J Rayman, R. Greenwald. *Oracle Data Warehousing and Business Intelligence Solutions.* Indianapolis, IN: Wiley Publishing, 2007.

Stackowiak, Robert. *Remaining Relevant in Your Tech Career.* New York, NY: Apress (Springer Media), 2019.

Online Sources

Basford, Tessa and Bill Schaninger (The Four Building Blocks of Change):
www.mckinsey.com/business-functions/organization/our-insights/the-four-building-blocks--of-change

Connelly, Mark (The Kurt Lewin Change Management Model):
www.change-management-coach.com/kurt_lewin.html

Dawson, Ryan (What would machine learning look like if you mixed in DevOps):
www.theregister.co.uk/2020/03/07/devops_machine_learning_mlops/

Design Council methodology (Double Diamond approach): www.designcouncil.org.uk/news-opinion/what-framework-innovation-design-councils-evolved-double-diamond

Design Management Institute (and design value): www.dmi.org/page/2015DVIandOTW/2015-dmiDesign-Value-Index-Results-and-Commentary.htm

Drahun, Gena (Average time to reach UX maturity):
www.linkedin.com/pulse/wicked-truth-ux-maturity-gena-drahun

Erb, Dillon (CI/CD for Machine Learning & AI):
https://blog.paperspace.com/ci-cd-for-machine-learning-ai/

Forbes (Design Thinking Comes of Age): https://hbr.org/2015/09/design-thinking-comes-of-age

Guru99 (Prototyping Model in Software Engineering): www.guru99.com/software-engineering-prototyping-model.html

IDEO Design Thinking methodology: https://designthinking.ideo.com/

IDEO Design Thinking training: www.ideou.com/

Information Age (survey of C-Suite executives re: Fortune 500):
www.information-age.com/65-c-suite-execs-believe-four-ten-fortune-500-firms-wont-exist-10-years-123464546/

Kotter, John (8-step process for leading change):
www.kotterinc.com/8-steps-process-for-leading-change/

La Torre, JP (Microservices: The Good, the Bad, and the Ugly):
https://dzone.com/articles/microservices-the-good-the-bad-and-the-ugly

Liedtka, Jeanne (Harvard Business Review – Why Design Thinking Works):
https://hbr.org/2018/09/why-design-thinking-works

Lindsey, Lora (LinkedIn – The 4 Pillars of a Value Framework):
www.linkedin.com/pulse/how-improve-your-business-case-technology-investments-lindsey-mba/

Nagji, Bansi & Geoff Tuff (Harvard Business Review – Managing Your Innovation Portfolio):
https://hbr.org/2012/05/managing-your-innovation-portfolio

Nielsen, Jakob (UX Maturity Stages): www.nngroup.com/articles/ux-maturity-stages-1-4/

Posta, Christian (The Real Success Story of Microservices Architectures):
https://blog.christianposta.com/microservices/the-real-success-story-of-microservices-architectures/

Prosci (assorted chain management articles):
www.prosci.com/resources/articles

Stanford Institute of Design: https://dschool.stanford.edu

Study.com (the brain and problem-solving): https://study.com/academy/lesson/the-brain-problem-solving-areas-process.html

Supply Chain Times (survey of 500 executives re: disruption):
https://sctimes.io/news/article/7/3831

Szczepanska, Jo (Design Thinking origin story): https://medium.com/@szczpanks/design-thinking-where-it-came-from-and-the-type-of-people-who-made-it-all-happen-dc3a05411e53

XPLANE Inspiration Landscape Worksheet:
https://x.xplane.com/inspiration_landscape_worksheet

Index

© Robert Stackowiak and Tracey Kelly 2020
R. Stackowiak and T. Kelly, *Design Thinking in Software and AI Projects*